THE NEWCOMER'S GUIDE TO HOME GARDENING IN NORTH AND CENTRAL FLORIDA

by
Karl M. Touraine

$13.95

First Printing

Library of Congress Card Number 92-71661

ISBN 0-9632916-0-2

Typesetting by Peirce Graphic Services, Inc., Stuart, FL 34997

Printed by Thomson-Shore, Inc., Dexter, MI 48130

F. R. Publications
8285 SW 107 Lane
Ocala, FL 34481

Cover photograph by Nancy Leonard of summer-color demonstration garden designed, planted and maintained by the Florida Master Gardeners of Marion County. Special thanks to Suzanne Shuffitt, Marion County Horticultural Assistant, for constant encouragement and factual information—to any number of Florida Master Gardeners of Marion County—and to two dear friends in Citrus County whose incessant questions kept me incessantly on my toes.

INTRODUCTION

Three years ago, my wife and I semi-retired from the lovely gardens of Wilton, Connecticut to a barrel of questions in Ocala, Florida.

We rented a nicely landscaped house in sight of where our own house was being built. When it was finished, we got the same landscaper to do his stuff on our place. It was expensive, but one of the best investments we made.

Almost the moment we moved in I stripped the sod from four plots measuring 53 feet, 13 feet, 32 feet and 67 feet, all by five feet wide—a total of 825 square feet, which I find is plenty.

We spread four or five yards of mostly-cow-manure topsoil on these sandy beds, piled about six inches high.

Into these beds, plus the landscaping, went over 80 varieties of annuals, perennials, vegetables, ornamentals and shrubs. Not all of them flourished. In addition, we've had maybe two dozen house and porch plants.

In the course of all this, it slowly dawned that gardening in Florida is really not that much different from gardening in Connecticut—with a few glaring exceptions. You have to relearn your seasons completely. You'll meet pretty much the same insects you know, plus a few new ones—but this part of Florida is far from the insect haven many northerners think it is. On the other hand, you'll meet fungi you never heard of, to be treated with fungicides you also never heard of.

I also believe starting things from seed in the garden is a whole lot chancier in Florida than up north. I suspect this is mostly a function of soil temperature and moisture.

I've tried to make what follows the most concise yet complete description of Florida gardening methods and problems I can. It's mostly based on information developed by the Institute of Food and Agricultural Sciences at the University of Florida, made available through our county Extension Service. To that I've added what I've learned from other veteran gardeners, plus my own experiences and observations—arranged subject by subject in alphabetical order.

Ocala, Florida
January, 1993

CONTENTS AT A GLANCE

BY CATEGORY

Animal Pests: Armadillos, Moles, Pocket Gophers

Bulbs, Corms, Tubers and Such: Amaryllis, Caladiums, Cannas, Crinum Lilies, Dahlias, Daylilies, Elephant Ears, Gladiolus, Narcissus, Society Garlic, Zephyr Lilies

Flowers: Alyssum, Bird-of-Paradise, Blue Daze, Calendula, Chrysanthemums, Cosmos, Dahlias, Daylilies, Geraniums, Gerbera Daisies, Gladiolus, Heather, Hollyhocks, Impatiens, Marigolds, Nicotiana, Pansies, Pentas, Periwinkle, Petunias, Phlox, Portulaca, Roses, Shasta Daisies, Snapdragons, Society Garlic, Zinnias.

Fruits: Apples, Bananas, Blueberries, Chicasaw Plums, Chilling Requirements, Citrus, Figs, Grapes, Loquats, Nectarines, Peaches, Pears, Pecans, Persimmons, Pineapples, Strawberries, Black Walnuts

Grass/Lawns: Bahia, Bermudagrass, Carpetgrass, Centipede, Chinchbugs, Fall Army Worms, Herbicides, Lawn Care, Mole Crickets, St. Augustine, Sod Webworms, Zoysia

Insects: Ants, Aphids, Beneficial, Chiggers, Chinchbugs, Cockroaches, Fall Army Worms, Fleas, Insect and Related Pest Control, Lace Bugs, Larvae, Love Bugs, Mealybugs, Mole Crickets, Nematodes, Nymphs, Pantry Pests, Scales, Scorpions, Sod Webworms, Termites, Thrips, Ticks, Wireworms

Ornamental and Other Shrubs: Azaleas, Boxwood, Camelias, Castorbeans, Crape Myrtle, Firethorn, Gardenias, Heather, Hibiscus, Hollies, Indian Hawthorn, Jasmine, Ligustrum, Nandina, Oleander, Pampas Grass, Photinia, Plumbago,

7

Podocarpus, Poinsettias, Roses, Sago Palms, Trumpet Vine, Wax Myrtle

Trees: Beech, Bottlebrush, Camphor, Cedar, Cherry Laurel, Chicasaw Plum, Chinese Tallow, Crabapple, Cypress, Dogwood, Elms, Eucalyptus, Golden Rain, Hackberry, Hollies, Jerusalem Thorn, Lichens, Loblolly Bay, Loquats, Magnolias, Maple (Red), Mistletoe, Mulberry, Oaks, Palms, Pines, Redbud, Silverbell, Spanish Moss, Sweet Gum, Sycamore, Tulip, Walnut, Wax Myrtle

Vegetables: Asparagus, Beans (Lima, Pole and Snap), Beets, Broccoli, Brussels Sprouts, Cabbage, Canteloupes, Carrots, Collards, Corn, Cucumber, Eggplant, Herbs, Lettuce, Mustard, Okra, Onions, Parsley, Peas (English and Southern), Peppers, Potatoes (White and Sweet), Radishes, Spinach, Squash (Summer and Winter), Tomatoes, Turnips, Watermelon

Miscellaneous: Chilling Requirements, Cold Protection, Diseases, Fertilizers, Ground Covers, Herbicides, Insect and Related Pest Control, Leaf Diagnosis, Lichens, Mistletoe, Mushroom Root Rot, Peat, Pruning, Soil pH, Sooty Mold, Spanish Moss, Sulfur

ALPHABETICALLY

Alyssum
Amaryllis
Ants
Aphids
Apples
Armadillos
Asparagus
Asparagus Fern
Azaleas
Bahiagrass
Bananas
Beans (Lima, Pole and Snap)
Beech, Blue
Beets
Beneficial Insects
Bermudagrass
Bird-of-Paradise
Blueberries
Blue Daze
Boring Insects
Bottlebrush
Boxwood
Broccoli
Brussels Sprouts

10 / Contents at a Glance

GEOGRAPHY

There are no hard and fast boundaries between north and central Florida, or between central and south.

Map 1 below is courtesy of the Florida Game and Fresh Water Fish Commission. Map 2 comes from the Florida Department of Agriculture and Consumer Services, Division of Forestry. Note the differences.

Other official definitions are 1) north is everything north and
west of Ocala, and central is from Ocala to Sebring, and 2)
north is north of State Road 40 (Yankeetown to Daytona
Beach), and central is from SR 40 to State Road 70 (Sarasota to
Fort Pierce). Best advice, when you live near the border, is do
as the natives do.

ALYSSUM

Listed as being tender, but I've had it down to 12° and still growing where it grew three years ago, requiring no care and producing big, fragrant blotches of white in amongst the potatoes, roses and summer squash. The white varieties—especially Carpet of Snow—do much better than the purple or lavender ones. The seed packet lists Carpet of Snow as an annual; maybe so, but it keeps growing year round—I guess from self-seeding.

AMARYLLIS

Do really well here, and you don't have to dig them up each fall. Best time to plant is October to February. If planting in a pot, leave half the bulb exposed; if in the ground, leave just the neck of the bulb exposed. Do best in partial shade. After a few years, they like to be transplanted to a rejuvinated bed. Bulb red-blotch is about their only disease—no cure, just dig them up and discard. Fertilize with 10-10-10 with micronutrients in spring before blooming, then a few months after blooming.

You can propagate amaryllis by cutting the bulb in vertical quarters (or even eighths if you wish) leaving a section of the bulb plate (that round thing on the bottom) on each section. Plant in perlite, keep in the dark and on the dry side.

We've had potted amaryllis on the terrace come back several years with no care whatsoever except water and occasional fertilizing.

ANTS

Florida boasts 14 common ant varieties, including three kinds of fire ants. They're related to the bees and wasps—and you can tell them from termites by their tiny waists and by the fact that their front pair of wings is much larger than the back pair; both the same size in the case of termites.

Male ants usually have wings, and their sole purpose is to mate, after which they die. Queen ants lose their wings after mating. Workers are seldom winged, vary a great deal in size and appearance. Their jobs are to construct, repair and defend the nest, to feed immature and adult ants including the queen, and to care for the brood.

Ants will eat almost anything, except they don't care for fabric or leather. They find food by random searching, and will travel long distances to find water.

Bites from imported fire ants can cause severe reactions which may require emergency hospitalization. Most other ant bites are just irritating unless you happen to be allergic. Note: I've found that aloe keeps fire ant bites from pustulating. Just break off a spine and rub the sap on the bite. But you have to do it right away, within minutes.

The key to eliminating house ants is cleanliness—just don't give them anything to eat. With yard ants, find the nest and treat with diazinon, Amdro, Dursban or sevin.

APHIDS

Aphids, sometimes called plant lice, have piercing mouth parts and cause damage by sucking out plant juices. Potentially even more damaging is their ability to transmit plant virus diseases.

Aphids have soft, pear-shaped bodies generally less than ⅛ inch long. They're usually green, but also come in black, brown, pink, yellow, blue and white. They like to cluster on stems and the undersides of leaves. Most are wingless, but when they've about finished off the plant they're feeding on, some develop wings and fly off to start new colonies.

Aphids are at their worst in early spring on the flush of new growth, but remain a problem year round. Curled or crinkled leaves suggest aphids; also honeydew, a sweet excretion that ants enjoy and that hosts a black fungus called sooty mold.

Biologically, most aphids are female. They reproduce without mating, and they seldom lay eggs. Instead, they give birth to live young. One female produces 50 to 100 daughters during her life span, and each daughter starts reproducing in just six to eight days—which means that every week you have a whole new generation to deal with.

Fortunately, control is not difficult. You can often dislodge aphids with a forceful stream from the garden hose. Or you can spray them with a soap solution of two tablespoons of liquid dishwashing detergent per gallon of water. The soap erodes the aphid's cuticle layer, and vital internal moisture is lost.

You can also kill aphids with diazinon and malathion, but a word of caution. Tiny wasp-like parasites prick tiny holes in aphids and deposit their eggs. When the egg hatches, the larva destroys the aphid. When you spray with strong insecticides, you kill these beneficial parasites and thus destroy highly desirable natural control.

APPLES

The further north you are, the better your chances with apples, which need a certain amount of cold to do well. South of Leesburg, chancy.

Apples also need another apple tree to cross-pollinate with. Fortunately, two recently developed varieties bloom at the same time (in the Gainesville area, anyway) and do well with a chill factor of 300 to 400 hours (see Chilling Requirement). They are Anna and Dorset Golden. A third variety grows well in northern Florida—Ein Shemer—but cross-pollination is more of a problem.

Apples grow best in sandy-loamy soil, but do reasonably well in other soils, too. Keep bare-root roots from drying out and plant, ideally, between late December and February. Container trees do well at any time of year provided they get enough water.

Mulch two feet around the tree to control weeds. Fertilize during the dormant season (January) and again in June, when hopefully the rainy season begins. Use a 10-10-10 at the rate of about half a pound for each year of the tree's age up to a maximum of seven pounds per application.

During dry periods you may have to water as frequently as every 10 days—more if you have very sandy soil. A big tree may need as much as 50 gallons of water, a small one maybe only five to ten gallons, in the area beneath the canopy.

Young apple trees should be pruned to leave five or six limbs to form the basic framework. The more perpendicular to the tree, the better. Space as evenly as possible around the trunk and six to eight inches up and down. Later pruning will be to remove deadwood and suckers, and to maintain shape.

Apples should be allowed to ripen on the tree, though immature fruit will also ripen satisfactorily in the refrigerator. Anna apples will hold up to six or eight weeks in the refrigerator.

A certain amount of preventive pest control is necessary for top quality trees and fruit.

Apple scab (which affects leaves, flowers and fruit) and bitter rot (which affects only the fruit) can be controlled with Captan or other suitable fungicide. When fireblight is present, cut out the dead branches and burn them—and cut down on the nitrogen. For scale insects, spray with a 3% oil solution during the dormant season—around mid-January. In winter, rabbits like to eat apple tree bark—keep them away with hardware cloth or a plastic tree guard around the trunk.

For more specific information, consult your garden store or county agent.

ARMADILLOS

If some morning you find a lot of trowel-like holes in your lawn or flowerbed, chances are it's an armadillo. These strange creatures feed on insects and invertebrates such as ants, grubs and earthworms, plus an occasional berry or mushroom. They normally live in burrows up to 15 feet long in woods or dense shaded places—but sometimes, where the feeding is good, they'll dig a short escape burrow and move in for a while—and there's not much you can do about it. They have no front teeth, so they can't bite—but their claws more than make up for that. The Marion County Game and Fresh Water Fish office has an armadillo trap they'll lend you, but so far it hasn't caught a single armadillo. Armadillos may not look it, but they're good runners and swimmers—and can even walk underwater to cross small streams. Another oddity: armadillos always have four young, born in February or March, and they're always identical and of the same sex.

ASPARAGUS

Not well adapted to Florida. It gets no dormant period, so growth is more or less constant, resulting in weak, spindly spears and wearing out in four or five years. Set crowns six to eight inches deep, 12 inches apart in rich soil. One way to go at it is to dig yourself a compost pit, and when it's full plant your asparagus in it. Mary Washington, Martha Washington, Reading Giant and Palmetto are recommended varieties.

AZALEAS

As an ornamental shrub, azaleas are at the top of the list on both counts—as a flowering ornamental, and an evergreen shrub. They bloom from late February (earlier if you plant the Krume hybrids) to early April (later with thc Satsuki hybrids). They do best in filtered sunlight, don't like dense shade, and do surprisingly well in full sun. They're shallow-rooted and need good drainage (and frequent watering). Above all, they need acid—really acid, pH 4.5 to 5.5—soil. So you'll probably want to amend our sandy Florida soil with peat moss, compost or pine bark (all help hold moisture) and wettable sulfur at the rate of one pound (no more) per 100 square feet of bed when you plant and two or three (at most) times per year. November to February is best planting time, but you can put in container plants anytime.

Frequent, light applications of an acid-forming 6-6-6 or 8-8-8 are recommended just after blooming and also in the summer, fall and winter—about a double handful, or half a pound, for a mature plant.

Pruning is best done right after blooming. After July or August, pruning won't hurt the plant, but it will cut down on next year's blooms.

Azaleas want to be mulched and should be watered twice a week during dry, windy spells. They are occasionally attacked by insects and/or disease, but usually not seriously. One local nursery recommends two ounces Volck oil plus a little copper sulfate per gallon of water four times a year.

When it comes to cultivars, the University of Florida lists 19 for central Florida plus another 15 for north Florida. Best bet is to consult your County Agent regarding color, size, bushiness, etc.

BAHIAGRASS

The University of Florida's FLORIDA LAWN CARE shows the advantages of bahiagrass as: It can be grown from seed, which is abundant and relatively unexpensive. Once established, bahia develops an extensive root system which makes it one of the most drought tolerant lawngrasses. Bahia produces a very durable sod which is able to withstand moderate traffic. In addition, bahia has fewer pest problems than any other Florida lawngrass, although mole crickets can severely damage it.

The principal disadvantages of bahiagrasses are the relatively open growth and the tall, unsightly (they're not really that unsightly) seedheads produced continuously from May through November. The prolific seed stalks, plus the very tough leaves and stems, make bahia difficult to mow. Weekly mowing with a heavy duty rotary mower is needed for best appearance. The coarse texture of bahia is often not appreciated. Bahia is not well suited to soils having a high pH, and grows poorly in areas subject to salt spray. Bahia often appears yellow due to lack of iron, and it can be severely damaged by mole crickets. Bahia also has low tolerance to currently available postemergence herbicides, which makes weed control difficult. Generally, bahia will not provide as nice a lawn as St. Augustine, which tends to produce a darker green, denser turf. If a crab-apple-green lawn with lower density is not acceptable, better choose something other than bahia.

BANANAS

You occasionally see banana trees in the Ocala area, but they are definitely not recommended for north Florida.

Bananas thrive best in humid, subtropical places out of the wind. 28° F can badly damage them, even kill them to the ground. However, new growth usually sprouts from the underground rhizome when warm weather returns. They grow fast, and some trees get quite large—until next year's cold kills them back again. Some even bear bananas.

If you're dead set to have a banana, fertilize with a couple of pounds of a 6-2-12 (or as close as you can find to that ratio) every couple of months. When it freezes back, cut back to a foot or two above the ground.

To harvest bananas, cut the stalk when the bananas are the right size, but before they turn yellow, put in a plastic bag and hang until they ripen.

BEANS, Lima

March-August north; February-April and again in September central. As with other beans, half the usual fertilizer and no need for inoculated seed. Stinkbugs can be a problem with limas—they injure the beans in the pods. Fordhook 242, Henderson, Jackson Wonder, Dixie, Butterpea—and pole varieties Florida Butter and Sieva.

BEANS, Pole

March-April and August-September north; February-April and August-September central. As with bush beans, half the usual fertilizer and no need for inoculated seed. Dade, McCasian, Kentucky Wonder 191, Blue Lake.

BEANS, Snap

A two-season crop. March-April and August-September in the north; February-April and September central. Fertilize at about half the rate for other vegetables. No need for inoculated seed in most soils. Varieties: Bush Blue Lake, Contender, Roma, Harvester, Provider, Cherokee Wax.

BLUE BEECH

Also called Water Beech, though it's not a beech at all, but the American Hornbeam; also known as Ironwood because of its muscular-appearing dark-grey trunk. (To confuse matters even further, there's also another Ironwood that sometimes uses the alias Hop Hornbeam). Anyway, this ironwood (*Carpinus caroliniana*, if you're talking to a nurseryman) is a small (25 to 30 feet) native of north and central Florida—an overlooked tree that does well in shade or full sun, on all but the most excessively drained soils, and has no pests to speak of.

BEETS

Strictly a cold season vegetable. September-March in north Florida, October-March central. Seeds need watering almost daily for good germination. My favorite variety is Long Season Winter Keeper. Early Wonder, Detroit Dark Red and Cylindra are also recommended.

BENEFICIAL INSECTS

Less than one of every 200 insects is a plant pest, and many of the others do us the favor of eating the pests. Among the more common of these beneficials are lady beetles (I always called them bugs, but here they're beetles), praying mantis, assassin bugs, aphid lions, ichneumon flies, ground beetles, serphid flies and several of the stinkbugs. Spiders pitch in by feeding on many insect pests, and not all mites are bad: some of them eat the bad ones.

Perhaps the most beneficial of all is a group of tiny wasp-like parasites who deposit their eggs in aphids, scales and whitefly nymphs. If you see a small hole in any of these, as if stuck with a straight pin (a 10 × magnifying glass is helpful),they've been parasitized—in which case, go easy on insecticides which kill the good guys with the bad.

More and more, we seem to be getting away from chemical control of insects and relying more on beneficial insects, also a bacterium that controls caterpillars, soaps instead of poisons (for soft-bodied insect pests) and a coming group of oil sprays that can be used in hot weather. Citrus blackfly is now under complete biological control thanks to two tiny, introduced wasps.

BERMUDAGRASS

Reading from the Florida Cooperative Extension Service's FLORIDA LAWN CARE, Bermudagrass's advantages are that it produces a vigorous, dark green, dense turf that is well adapted to most soils and climatic regions in Florida. It has excellent wear, drought and salt tolerance. It establishes rapidly and is competitive against weeds.

On the negative side, Bermudagrass has a large number of cultural and pest problems which restrict its use in many Florida situations. It is not suitable for most home lawns because of the need for restricted-use pesticides to control nematodes and insects. It requires the most maintenance for an acceptable appearance of any Florida turfgrass.

In central and north Florida, Bermudagrass turns brown in cold weather, has very poor shade tolerance and is susceptible to several nematode, insect and disease problems. Due to its rapid growth nature, thatch buildup can be a problem. A reel mower should be used to produce the highest possible quality turf stand.

I've seen a lawn book that touts Bermudagrass as the bellwether grass for warm climates. I'll put my money on the University of Florida.

BIRD-OF-PARADISE

You can grow this relative of the banana outdoors in parts of central Florida, and in bring-in-when-cold containers in the rest of north and central Florida. The critical temperature is 24° F, which it can withstand for a short time.

Blooming time is September through May. Any soil will do, but rich loam is best, and good drainage is essential. Plants in partial shade will grow taller and have slightly larger flowers than full-sun plants. Plant no deeper than soil level, be generous with water and mulch.

Every three months during the growing season, fertilize with four pounds of a slow release such as sludge or bloodmeal per 100 square feet, or two pounds of 6-6-6. Minor elements are recommended. Bird-Of-Paradise is relatively free of, but not immune to, pests and disease, so keep your eyes open.

Divide clumps in late spring or early summer. Remove dead leaves and roots, and soak in one part household bleach to ten parts water for 10 minutes to prevent any disease or pest carry-over. It will be three months or more before roots become established, at which time commence fertilizing.

BLUEBERRIES

If your soil is very acid (pH 3.5 to 5.2) and you have a taste for fruit-flavored muffins, blueberries may be for you. Even if your pH is higher (but not over 6.5), there's a way out.

Choose a sunny spot away from all tree roots (pine is ok) and 20 feet from your house (so foundation lime won't raise pH). Space planting holes four feet or more. Put ¼ cubic foot of Canadian peatmoss (½ cubic foot if pH over 5.2) in the bottom of each hole and around the roots.

Best planting time is December 20 to February 20. Choose plants about two feet high with well-developed (but not pot-bound) roots. Keep bareroot roots moist, but don't soak. With container plants, the root ball should be thoroughly broken up and the roots spread in the hole. Keep plants heavily mulched with pine straw, pine bark or oak leaves—but no grass clippings.

Blueberries should be pruned at planting. Choose the tallest, strongest stem and leave it alone. Prune back the other stems and any twiggy growth at the bottom of the plant. First-year flowers should be stripped off (be sure to wear gloves) to promote vigorous growth.

Blueberries respond well to light, frequent fertilization; an overdose of fertilizer can actually kill them. You can get a special blueberry fertilizer in Florida, and it's recommended. Give new plants just an ounce per plant over a two-foot circle around the stem. Repeat in April, June, August and October. If plants are heavily mulched, increase the dose to 1½ ounces. Next year, go up to 2 ounces over a three-foot circle, then 3 ounces in the third year. After that, play it by instinct.

Throughout north and central Florida, the highbush Sharpblue variety is recommended. This early producer usually ripens May 1 to May 15 south of Ocala and May 10 to 25 north of it. Other varieties (there are lots of them, and they're all called rabbit-eye as opposed to highbush) include Bonita, Beckyblue, Climax, Premier, Brightwell, Powderblue, Choice, Chaucer, Woodard and Bluebelle. These are generally not recommended south of Ocala, so you might check with your county agent before trying them.

BLUE DAZE

I haven't grown this myself, but it's a lovely spreading perennial that seems to grow beautifully in the border or in foundation planting. Has a long blooming period.

BORING INSECTS

Florida has no dearth of insects whose larvae burrow into trees and shrubs, doing them no good. They usually attack plants that have been stressed by something else—injury, drought, soil compaction, soil added or taken away above the roots, digging too near, lightning, winds, wounds caused by vehicles or machinery such as weed eaters.

Dogwoods, redbuds, magnolias and pines are especially susceptible—but we also have peach tree borers, Australian pine borers, ash borers, red oak borers, etc., etc.

Prevention is the best control against borers; the healthier the plant, the less open to damage. Protective sprays usually don't work, but if you have a particularly desirable shrub or tree that's been injured, you can try spraying it with lindane every four months or Dursban every two months.

The usual signs of borers are boring dust and/or sap at the entry holes. If you see these, and the plant is still healthy, spray with lindane or Dursban and cross your fingers. If the plant is not healthy, best consider removing it—no need for a source of borers to infect other, nearby plants.

Some of the larger borers can be controlled after they've entered the tree. Squirt or spray lindane or Dursban into the holes and seal them with putty. In some cases, a long wire can be pushed into the hole to kill the larva.

If you notice the tips of shoots or branches wilting in the spring, chances are you've got twig borers. Prune infected tips and burn them as soon as possible.

BOTTLEBRUSH

A cheerful, small (to 20 feet) tree that brightens the landscape wherever it's planted. Medium rate of growth. Evergreen. Leaves are slender, narrow, pointed—and have a spicy aroma. Flowers are brilliant red and look like bottlebrushes. Two common varieties: erect and branching; and weeping. Tolerant of poor soil and drought, but—around Ocala, anyway— wants to be planted in a cold-protected spot. Principal pests are scales, stem gall and mushroom root rot.

BOXWOOD

Evergreen, needs little or no fertilizing, takes pruning and shaping beautifully, does well in almost any soil with a pH range of 5.5 to 7.4, likes full sun to partial shade and is extremely cold hardy. Left to itself, grows globe-like to a height of six to 25 feet. The ideal plant for topiary.

BROCCOLI

August-February north, August-January central. Although a cool season vegetable, prolonged frost can kill or stunt it. Keep harvesting side shoots after the main head is cut. Recommended varieties are Early Green Sprouting, Waltham 29, Atlantic, Green Comet and Green Duke.

BRUSSELS SPROUTS

October-December both north and central. Need cold weather for best growth—and some freezing for best taste. Remove leaves as sprouts grow up the stalk. Recommended are Jade Cross and Long Island Improved.

BULBS

Florida offers a wide choice of bulbous plants that will produce beautiful flowers and foliage year after year—but they're not the same bulbous plants you may be used to. We just don't get cold enough for tulips and daffodils (though paperwhites do well), crocuses and hyacinths, snowdrops and scylla—unless you treat them as annuals.

Instead, we offer amaryllis, caladium, callas, cannas, dahlias, daylilies, elephant ears, gladioli, paperwhites and society garlic, and many, many more—for some of which be warned you have to be an avid gardener and enjoy working.

For more details, see your County Extension Agent or a nurseryman.

CABBAGE

September-February north, September-January central. Buy clean plants to avoid cabbage black-rot, a common bacterial disease that causes yellow patches on leaf margins. And keep an eye out for loopers. Gourmet, Marion Market, King Cole, Market Prize, Red Alice, Chieftan Savoy, Rio Verde and Bravo are all recommended.

CALADIUMS

Among the most colorful of all foliage plants, with a wide choice of pinks, reds, whites and greens in lots of different combinations and patterns.

Available as tubers, seedlings or full-sized plants. If you buy tubers, the bigger the tuber the bigger the leaves will be. Avoid soft, spongy tubers—usually a sign of frost damage.

Caladiums will grow year-round in more southerly parts of central Florida, though you may get some dieback in cold

snaps. In northern Florida, you'll probably do best by lifting tubers in the fall and replanting them in early May.

Many caladiums are derived from Amazon basin plants used to rich, well-aerated, moist soil—so peat moss, manure or compost is in order, especially if your soil is sandy. They respond to partial shade with larger, more colorful leaves, but do ok in sun. They'll appreciate a little 8-8-8 five weeks or so after planting and every other month thereafter—or monthly if your soil is really sandy and easily leachable. Insects and diseases shouldn't be much problem provided you don't let the tubers get below 60° F—which would take more than just a one-night cold stand, considering the tubers are in the ground.

One word of warning: Caladiums don't like to be splashed, so don't plant them under un-guttered eaves, and mulch to keep down rain-splattered soil damage.

CALENDULA

A hardy plant which makes an excellent spring flower; I've even had a few that made it through the winter. Plant February-March north, November-February central for beautiful blooms through June. Also known as the Pot Marigold, whose flower it resembles.

CAMELLIAS

If I had a semi-shaded (ideally by pine trees) area, camellias are probably the first thing I'd plant in it. Fall-to-winter blooming Sasanqua types and winter-to-spring Japonicas will give you blooms from October to March. The foliage is a deep, lustrous evergreen. Camellias like well-drained, acid soil, but not as acid as many people think—a pH of 5.8 to 6.2 is fine.

You'll want to fertilize in early spring, when new growth starts; in late April or May; in mid-summer; and once again in late fall or early winter. 6-6-6 is good at the rate of two pounds per 100 square feet applied around the plant out to the drip line. Mulching pays good dividends. Spray twice with Kelthane or equivalent, seven to 10 days apart, in March; again, lightly, in late June and late September. Paint an inch-wide band of Cygon around the trunk below the lowest branch in April. And check the leaf undersides regularly for tea scale, which is very small, whitish and shaped like a thin rod. Cut blooms regularly, and prune when blooming is over.

Camellias grow five to 15 feet tall and come in so many flower variations that the only way to choose is to see the plants in bloom. Best planting time is November to February, so that roots can establish themselves before summer heat arrives.

CAMPHOR TREE

A beautiful, smallish (not over 40 to 50 feet), wide spreading evergreen. It grows here in Ocala, but runs into problems when the temperature dips to 15° or so. Source of camphor, as you can tell if you crush a leaf. Likes sandy loam, but isn't that particular.

CANNA LILIES

Or just plain cannas. And it's a pity they aren't grown more widely. They come from 16 inches to six feet tall, your choice of scarlet, yellow, gold, salmon, orange, pink, coral and rose flowers, with copper, green, bronze or red foliage—though not necessarily in all combinations.

They grow from fleshy, underground rhizomes and can be grown most of the year in both north and central Florida. They prefer well-drained, loamy soil rich in organic matter and containing abundant nutrients—but in fact will grow in almost any soil given fertilization and irrigation.

Plant dwarf cultivars (16 to 18 inches tall) about a foot apart, and two feet apart for tall (up to six feet) varieties. Low growing (two to three feet) varieties are also available. Full sun or semi-shade.

Flowers are borne on stems, and when the flowers wither, prune off the stem, and you'll most likely get a new flowering stem. Keep repeating this (sometimes for as many as four flowering stems) and you can have canna flowers for most of the summer. When you get no more flowering stems, cut everything back to ground level or slightly above.

Cannas thrive in hot summer sun—provided adequate water and fertilizer. In absence of rain, water twice a week. Fertilize in early spring with 10-10-10 and then monthly at the rate of about one pound per 100 square feet. If your fertilizer contains 20 percent nitrogen, cut the dose to half a pound; if five percent, up it to two pounds.

Come cold weather, and you may want to lift the rhizomes, dry them for a week or so (but not in full sun), trim the dried roots and store in peat moss (with ventilation—not air-tight) until spring.

Canna leaves are coated with a water-repellant wax, so disease is not much of a problem. But keep an eye out for grasshoppers and caterpillars.

CANTALOUPES

March-April north, February-April central. Bees needed for pollination. Space-taking—up to six feet between rows, three feet between vines. Smith's Perfect, Ambrosia, Edisto 47, Planters Jumbo, Summet and Super Market are recommended varieties.

CARPETGRASS

Again turning to the Extension Service's FLORIDA LAWN CARE, carpetgrass's advantages are that it will grow on wet soil where few other grasses persist, and has moderate shade tolerance. It is low-growing and produces a dense turf with good color when fertilized. Carpetgrass can also be grown from seed.

Against that, carpetgrass will not survive on very dry soils unless irrigated frequently. Roots tend to be very shallow, so this grass has poor drought tolerance. During the summer it produces numerous tall, thin seedheads which make the lawn unattractive unless mowed frequently. It also has poor cold hardiness, turning brown with the first cold spell, and is slow to green up in the spring. The texture is medium, the color light green and salt tolerance poor. It is troubled by several insects, diseases and nematodes. It is also recommended to be grown only in acid (pH 5-5.5) soils.

Carpetgrass is not recommended for a high-quality lawn— however, it can be used in wet, shady areas where ease of maintenance is more important than quality.

CARROTS

Another cool season vegetable. Plant September-March in north Florida, October-March in central. Imperator, Chantenay, Nantes, Gold Pak, Waltham Hicolor and Orlando Gold are recommended varieties. Do best in a raised bed.

CASTORBEANS

If you want a large (up to 10 feet), lush, fast growing, tree-like (it's actually a herb) plant as a screen or backdrop, the castorbean is for you. Around here, it dies back in winter, and best procedure is to save some of the many seeds it puts out, pull out the old plant and start over next spring. The plants, and especially the seeds, are poisonous.

CEDAR, SOUTHERN RED

A fast-growing native often used for soil stabilization, as an accent tree, and sometimes as a Christmas tree. Likes full sun and alkaline soils. Both sexes produce small, blue-green cones that attract wildlife. An aromatic conifer with a conical shape. Up to 30 feet. Subject to juniper blight, mushroom root rot and cedar apple rust.

CENTIPEDEGRASS

Again from the University of Florida's FLORIDA LAWN CARE, centipedegrass is adapted to infertile soils. It spreads by stolons, producing a medium-textured turf. Maintenance requirements are low when compared to other turfgrasses. It has fair to good shade tolerance, good drought tolerance, and can be established from seed.

On the negative side, centipedegrass is highly susceptible to damage from nematodes and ground pearl insects. It exhibits iron chlorosis (yellowing) and produces a heavy thatch if over-fertilized. It has poor salt tolerance and will not withstand heavy foot traffic.

If overfertilized and overwatered, centipedegrass will, in several years, develop large brown dead spots in early spring—known as "centipedegrass decline"—a problem that can be prevented by caution not to overfertilize, preventing thatch accumulation, irrigating during drought stress (especially in the fall) and maintaining a mowing height of one and a half to two inches.

CHERRY LAUREL

Can grow up to 30 feet, but mostly used as a hedge or specimen shrub. It takes to pruning and shaping almost as well as boxwood, and in spring puts out pale yellowish-green leaves that are most attractive. Native, evergreen and fast growing. It's a true cherry, *Prunus caroliniana*—where it picked up the laurel part of its name I haven't a clue.

CHICKASAW PLUM

Native to north and central Florida, where you often see them in spring bloom on hummocks and along fence rows. Up to 30 feet. Large, snowy white blooms in late winter—bright green, lustrous foliage—shiny red or yellow plums about half an inch in diameter (yes, you can make jam out of them if you wish). Deciduous, medium to fast grower. A hardy, flowering landscape tree you'd expect to see more frequently. Will grow in most soils, though prefers rich and fertile. Caterpillars the major pest.

CHIGGERS

Chiggers are tiny ($\frac{1}{50}$ inch) mite larvae which usually like low, damp places with heavy vegetation, but also occur in dry places, and sometimes even on lawns. The mother mite usually lays all her eggs in one place, so chiggers tend to occur in pockets or bunches. They get on your skin and inject a fluid which dissolves tissue, which they feed upon. Four to eight hours later, you get an intense itch and, most likely, welts that can last up to two weeks.

Chiggers like body parts where clothing fits tightly or the skin is thin, tender or wrinkled—like waistlines, ankles and knees. They're easily removed by taking a hot bath or shower and lathering up several times. You can get temporary relief from the itching with a local, nonprescription anesthetic—also, so says the Journal of the American Medical Association, by rubbing meat tenderizer into the welts.

If you're going where chiggers may be, protective clothing is a good idea, and also repellents containing (for instance) DEET. Dusting sulfur will also repel chiggers.

You can test for chigger presence by placing a piece of black cardboard edgewise on the ground. If chiggers are present, you'll see tiny little yellow or pink dots climb to the top of the cardboard and congregate. Diazinon or Dursban is in order.

CHILLING REQUIREMENT

Apples, peaches, pears and most other fruits which originated in temperate zones require a winter dormancy period so they can rest, after which they gather up their juices and start the new season.

Temperatures below 45° F (7° C) are known as chilling temperatures and are measured in hours. The Florida Panhandle rarely gets less than 500 chilling hours; south central Florida may get as few as 200.

A plant that doesn't get enough chilling hours of rest is often erratic in the way it leafs out and blooms, and tends not to live long. A plant that gets more rest than it needs often starts growing with the first warm spell, only to get klunked by a far from uncommon late frost.

To find out the number of chilling hours for your particular location, and the plants that do well within this range, call your county extension agent.

CHINCH BUGS

If your St. Augustine lawn is developing big, brown areas, especially along concrete or asphalt edges, could well be chinch bugs. They're only a fifth of an inch or less, reddish to black (the older the blacker) with a white band across the back. It's easy to check for them—one and a half ounces liquid dishwashing detergent (the kind you use by hand, not the machine kind) to a two-gallon watering can, sprinkle over four square feet, and if you have chinch bugs you'll know it in about two minutes—also whether you have any mole crickets or lawn caterpillars. April to September is the usual season, and diazinon or Dursban the usual control.

CHINESE TALLOW

Also called the popcorn tree—when its seeds ripen in the fall, they split open and look so much like popcorn you might want to sew them into a chain—which you can. These seeds have a waxy coating containing a tallow-like substance (hence the name) once used to make soap and candles. A fast-growing, not too tall tree with bright red fall color. One of the increasingly most popular (in the Ocala area, anyway) trees for the home landscape.

CHRYSANTHEMUMS

Periodically the garden stores overflow with beautiful, healthy, inexpensive mums which you soon see scattered in garden after garden. I've always considered chrysanthemums labor intensive, and they're even more so here. They like a bed that has three or four inches of organic matter and two pounds of 6-6-6 per 100 square feet tilled in to about six inches. Allow 18 to 30 inches between plants, depending on how vigorous. When they're established and six inches or taller, pinch off the top one or two inches to encourage lateral branching and produce lower, bushier plants. When lateral branches get six to eight inches, pinch them, too. Come August, no more pinching—they need a certain amount of stem length for buds and flowers.

Next spring, divide the clumps to prevent overcrowding and weak, spindly growth. Discard the center shoots—may have crown root fungus. Plant as above, give them one pound of 6-6-6 per 100 square feet two or three times—and then back to pinching.

Cyprus Gardens has the gardeners to do what chrysanthemums need—and the results are breath-taking.

CITRUS

If you live south of Leesburg, you can probably grow citrus without too much cold damage—though there will be days you'll wish you'd settled south of Orlando.

Here in Ocala, one neighbor has no trouble growing oranges—while others swear never again.

Citrus is well worth trying. It has shiny, evergreen leaves, bears beautiful flowers and delicious fruits, and is comparatively trouble-free.

Draw a line from the mouth of the Suwannee River through Gainesville to Green Cove Springs, then up the St. Johns River to the ocean. If you live south of the line and north of Leesburg/Orlando, here's the recommended procedure:

1. Choose the right citrus variety. Kumquats and satsuma (a tangerine-like mandarin orange, the most widely grown citrus in Japan) are the two most cold-hardy, edible citrus. Ideally, they'll be grafted onto trifoliate root-stock, though sour orange is also recommended.

2. Select a good planting site. Cold air drains downhill, so higher elevations beat lower ones. Plant to the south or southeast of your house: it will serve as a windbreak from freezing north and northwest winds, forcing them up and over the house, and over the citrus as well.

3. Keep soil around citrus completely free of weeds, grass and mulch, especially during cold weather. Grass and mulch act as soil insulators, prevent solar heat from entering the soil by day for release during the night. Also, moist soil will absorb more heat than dry soil—so water your citrus thoroughly two or three days before a freeze is expected.

4. No fertilizing, insecticides or pruning (the latter two are seldom needed anyway) after September 15—so that trees can harden off before winter comes. When a freeze is expected, bank surrounding soil to cover the graft bud and lower trunk of trees that have been in for only three to five years. You can also cover smaller trees with blankets, paper or other materials—just be sure to remove them in the morning.

The further south you go, the fewer precautions needed. Also, the wider your choice of citrus.

After kumquats and satsuma, the order of hardiness goes tangerines, oranges (especially navel, Hamlin and Parson Brown), grapefruits, lemons and limes.

For varities that do well in your area, best bet is to call your county extension service or to consult your nurseryman.

Citrus Culture

On the whole, citrus doesn't require that much care.

Most dooryard (the term down here for home garden) citrus comes in containers (as opposed to bare roots) and you can plant it any time, though late winter and early spring are best.

Remove all grass and weeds in a two to three foot circle. If your soil is poorly drained, build mounds 18 to 24 inches high and 12 feet in diameter, and plant on them. Sandy soil needs little or no special preparation. Soil pH should be kept between 6 and 7.

Plant trees 20 to 25 feet apart. No need to mulch—citrus is one of the few Florida crops that doesn't care for mulching.

Fertilize three times a year—Jan.–Feb., May–June and late Aug.– early Sept.—with a 6-6-6 containing magnesium, manganese and copper minors.

No need to prune except to shape the tree or remove suckers.

Insect and disease control can be very complicated or very simple—take your choice. Several insects, mites and fungus diseases may render fruit a trifle unsightly, but have little effect on internal quality, and the recommended procedure is to ignore them. If you do decide to put in a spray program, best to see your county agent for help.

Citrus ripens only on the tree—pick it too soon, and it will never ripen.

COCKROACHES

Also called waterbugs, croton bugs and palmetto bugs. They destroy food and damage fabrics, bookbindings and other materials. They have an oily secretion that smells terrible, makes food unappetizing, can even make apparently clean dishes smell bad. On top of that, they can spread disease, and allergic people become ill when roaches are present.

Common Florida varieties include Woods, American, Smoky-Brown, Brown, Australian and German. Size varies from ⅝ inch to two inches.

Roaches hide in dark places during the day, come out to feed at night. Look for them around the kitchen sink, in cracks around cupboards and cabinets, behind drawers, around pipes, behind loose baseboards, etc.

Best way to control roaches is to remove their food supply by good sanitation. You can spray chemical controls such as a 1% Baygon solution or ½% diazinon or Dursban into crevices where roaches hide. Other anti-roach products include dusts, baits and aerosol fogs.

Long range, there are several Insect-Growth-Regulator products that make immature cockroaches grow into sterile adults with twisted wings. As older roaches die, these take their place and no new young are born. Control takes six or seven months. You can get these IGR products either over the counter in your garden supply store or through a pest control operator.

COLD PROTECTION

When planting cold-sensitive plants, remember that cold air drains downhill and that generally the most protected areas are on the south and southeast sides of your house.

When a freeze is predicted, water around plants two or three days before it's due—moist soil absorbs more solar heat than does dry soil. Pull back mulch for increased heat absorption. Leave it pulled back for an overnight freeze; push it back for a longer freeze, to protect the roots. Tent to the ground with boxes, sheets, plastic, whatever, and include a light bulb. Don't let the covering (especially if it's plastic) touch the foliage, and remove it—or otherwise ventilate—when the sun comes out. If you have a lot of exposed flower pots or containers, push them together and/or mulch around them to protect the roots. Windbreaks will also offer some protection.

COLLARDS

Tolerates more heat than most other crucifers. February-March, then again August-November in the north; August-April in central. Harvest lower leaves as they mature. Georgia, Vales, Blue Max and Hicrop Hybrid are recommended.

CORN

Plant March-April and August in north; February-March and August-September in central. Wind is always a problem, partially solved by planting deep (2 + inches) and thinning to only 8 inches so the stalks can support each other. Takes more fertilizing, but less staking. The only variety I've tried is Silver Queen—which isn't the pure white Silver Queen of yore. Many ears didn't fill out, probably due to incomplete pollenization. Flea beetles, earworms and borers—the standard corn trio—have not been much of a problem. Recommendation is not to plant supersweet varieties along with standard varieties—the further apart in time and distance, the better.

COSMOS

We've had good luck with two kinds—the tall (usually need staking) Sensational and the smaller Klondyke varieties such as Bright Eyes. Other varieties such as Daydream, Gloria and Sonata haven't done well at all. Before the heat gets them, the Sensational are just that—and another flower not everyone here is familiar with. Bright Eyes gets about two feet high, yellow-gold to reddish—and has the happy habit of reseeding itself. When the plants fade, pull them. A whole new crop will soon follow—and next spring they'll come again with no help from anyone.

CRABAPPLE

This one is for north Florida only—a beautiful, little (up to 25 feet) native tree with white to pink, fragrant flowers in March. Deciduous. Medium to fast growing. Good in confined areas, or as a flowering landscape tree. Does best in rich, fertile soil—and away from any nearby cedars which could contribute to apple-cedar rust. Other pests are caterpillars and leaf spot fungi.

CRAPE MYRTLE

One of our most beautiful and useful shrubs/small trees. So-called because of its crape-like, crinkly flower clusters and its European myrtle-like leaves. Comes in dwarf (under three feet), semi-dwarf (three to six feet), medium (six to 12 feet) and large (12 to 20 feet)—drooping (new) or non-drooping—in many shades of white, pink, red and lavender.

The ideal time to plant is late spring or early summer when new blooms are emerging and you can see what you're getting. Full sun, and the more open the better for good air circulation. Almost any soil will do; loamy, slightly acidic is ideal. Mulch helps hold moisture and minimize soil temperature fluctuations. Deep-water new plants daily for at least two weeks, and then every other day for another two weeks—also, once a week at least during long, hot, dry spells when plants are growing and producing blooms. 6-6-6 or 8-8-8 in early spring (some authorities add late spring, summer and early winter) at the rate of one to two pounds per 100 square feet of planting bed.

Pruning is the key to vigorous, all-summer blooming. Prune small, twiggy growth to promote free air circulation, and prune branches back a foot or more to promote profuse blooming. Most people try to follow, rather than shape, the naturally pleasing form of crape myrtles. As flower clusters fade and turn to berries, snip them off so strength will go to new blooms and not to seeds—the more you do that, the longer your blooming season.

The reason for emphasizing free air circulation is to avoid powdery mildew, one of crape myrtle's comparatively few pest/disease problems. Others are aphids and whiteflies, which lead to another fungus, sooty mold. Benomyl is recommended for powdery mildew, Di-Syston or malathion for aphids and whiteflies and, for sooty mold, soap at three tablespoons per gallon of water—which, in fact, is also good against aphids and whiteflies.

Crape myrtle is sometimes called the Lilac of the South. It isn't a lilac, and it has no fragrance—but given that lilacs won't grow here (won't bloom, anyway) crape myrtles are welcome substitutes, and lovely plants in their own rights.

CRINUM LILY

A large, amaryllis-like lily with white to deep rose string-like flowers in spring and summer. Plant bulbs or offsets in winter—or, for that matter, any time of year you like. Leave the neck of the bulb above ground. Allow three feet between large (up to five foot) varieties. Full sun to partial shade. Soil should be well drained (though mature plants can survive flooding) and mulched. Makes a striking potted plant. As with amaryllis, leave half the bulb above soil level. Subject to red blotch, and should probably be dug up and replanted every few years. Crinum, incidentally, is a Greek word for lily.

CUCUMBERS

February-April and August-September north; February-March and September central. Bees needed for pollination. Some of the newer varieties produce all-female flowers (the ones that make the cucumbers); others produce both male and female flowers. Slicing varieties are Poinsett, Ashley, Sprint, Sweet Success and Pot Luck. Galaxy, SMR 18 and Explorer are picklers.

CYPRESS

Or Bald Cypress, if you prefer. One of our most beautiful native trees. Medium to fast growing (when young, anyway), 40 to 125 feet tall, will grow on most soils from lakeside-wet to upland-sandy—yet you hardly ever see it in the home landscape. Pity. Feathery, flat, juniper-like leaves fall in winter. Pests include leaf beetles and caterpillars.

DAHLIAS

Native to the uplands of Mexico and Guatamala, and can't survive the New England winter—so you'd think north and central Florida would be ideal for dahlias. Well, tain't. It's just too darned hot, and the plants begin to fade shortly after they start to bloom. Dahlias from seed seem to do a little better (if you can get them to germinate) and offer the side possibility of producing a new color, which you can then propagate through the tubers.

If you do try dahlias, you may want to take up the tubers after the foliage dies back—not because of freezing, but because they tend to rot.

DAYLILIES

One of our truly delightful perennials, and just as trouble-free as up north.

Best time to buy daylilies is when they're in bloom, so you

can see what you're getting. They come short, medium and tall—extra-early, early, mid and late blooming—evergreen, semi-evergreen and dormant—in yellows, reds, golds, oranges, peaches, pinks and purples, plus a number of variegated color combinations.

Growers recommend generous additions of peat, compost or other organic material, especially in sandy soil, when planting; pruning foliage back to four or five inches for easier handling and mulching (though almost nobody does this); and pruning dead flower stalks and foliage following bloom (which almost nobody does, either).

You can divide root clumps every two years or so for an ever-increasing supply of daylilies. They're not sensitive to heat, like full sun or partial shade, are generally pest and disease free, should be mulched, and appreciate late winter fertilizing plus one or two additional applications—ask your nursery for their recommendations.

Beyond a doubt, one of our best all-around plants.

DISEASES

.Plant diseases (as opposed to pest damage) are caused by fungi, bacteria, viruses and virus-related mycoplasmas, which are the smallest known (up til now, anyway) independently living organisms. Similar diseases can be caused by more than one of these pathogens, but in general: Fungi cause anthracnose, black spot, blight, canker, damping off, downy mildew, some leaf spots, leaf blights and wilts, powdery mildew, rusts and smuts. Bacteria cause fireblight, leaf spots, slime flux, some galls, leaf blights, rots, scabs and wilts. Viruses and mycoplasmas cause mosaic, stunt, some leaf spots, ring spots and yellows.

It takes three conditions to bring about a plant disease: 1) a pathogenic agent, 2) a susceptible host and 3) a favorable environment.

Pathogenic agents are everywhere and there is no possible

way to avoid them. Fungi spores are in the air by the millions. Wind, rain, insects, birds, snails, slugs, worms, transplant soil, contaminated tools, infected seed, pollen, even people—all can and do spread plant pathogens.

You have some control over the susceptible host. The healthier your plants, the more resistant to infection. Prune out sick or injured parts. Water and fertilize as needed to avoid stress. And try to find resistant varieties. Some root-stocks resist debilitating nematodes better than others. The "VFN" on some tomato seed packets indicates resistance to verticillium wilt, fusarium wilt and nematodes.

You also have some control over the environment. Water early in the day so plants (including grass) can dry with the early sun—high humidity and moisture favor fungi. Pull dead or diseased plants and burn or compost—ditto old plant debris. Prune dead foliage and branches. Don't plant the same thing in the same place two years in a row.

There is little or nothing you can use to combat virus diseases except practice good sanitation and procedures. The usual weapons against bacteria are chlorine (Clorox), steam-cleaning of equipment and streptomycin sulfate.

Most fungicides aren't cides, but rather preventatives—they don't kill, but ward off fungi or stop its growth. Daconil 2787, maneb and copper fungicide—plus maybe Funginex and benomyl so you don't keep using the same things all the time—should give you a pretty good anti-fungus arsenal.

DOGWOODS

You'll see lots of disappointing-looking dogwoods here in Florida—mostly because they're planted in the open when they're meant to be understory plants. Dogwood is native to Florida, and should do well when planted in the right place. One problem is the black twig borer, who lays eggs in the tips of branches, which the larvae then polish off. The pink variety, incidentally, just doesn't seem to grow here.

EGGPLANT

February-July north; January-March and August-September central. Plants are best staked, and you can expect to harvest well into summer. Recommended varieties are Florida Market, Black Beauty, Dusky, Long Tom, Ichiban and Tycoon.

ELEPHANT EARS

If you like large, tropical-looking leaves, these are for you. Some varieties get as tall as eight feet. Best time to plant is in the fall—four inches deep, two to four feet apart, and moist soil is essential. Full sun to light shade. They may be killed to the ground in winter in north Florida, but will come back. Further south, beware—they can take over your garden.

ELM, Drake

Very common in shopping malls and small commercial settings, and increasingly in home landscapes. Also known as Chinese elm, and (less frequently) as weeping elm. Semi-evergreen/semi-deciduous (depends on location and weather) with small, fine-textured foliage. An excellent choice wherever a small (up to 35 feet), fast-growing tree is needed. Blooms in small clusters late summer, early autumn. Not especially susceptible to pest damage.

ELM, Florida

Native to north and central Florida. Similar to the American elm, but much smaller at 40 to 50 feet. Best recognized by its inverted cone-shaped crown and large numbers of inconspicuous flowers preceding the leaves, which are deciduous. Grows best in wet hammocks and moist, fertile soils. Caterpillars the major pest.

ELM, Winged

50 to 75 feet, and also native to north and central Florida. A beautiful shade tree with an open, round-topped crown. And an excellent street or estate-lane choice. Prefers dry or well-drained soil, but is fairly adaptable. Deciduous, medium growth rate. No serious pests.

EUCALYPTUS

The Silver Dollar tree. 15 to 30 feet, with those small, silvery-bluish-gray, oval or heart-shaped leaves you see so often in floral arrangements. An Australian evergreen of medium rate growth. Has been grown as far north as near Jacksonville, but does best in central Florida. A good accent tree for patios and other confined areas. May need occasional shaping. Has no serious pest problems.

FALL ARMY WORMS

The moth is light brown with about a 1½ inch wingspan. Just-hatched caterpillars are grayish-green with stripes along the sides. As they eat your grass and grow to a length of 1½ inches, they become pale brown to black and the stripes along the sides becomes larger. An inverted, yellow "Y" on the front of the head all but guarantees identification.

Army worm (sometimes called fall army worm, but don't be fooled—they're usually among the first lawn caterpillars to show up) damage is similar to sod webworm, but more scattered than in patches. They feed during the day, and you can see them crawling on your grass.

As with sod webworms, good lawn management pays dividends, and insecticides make control relatively easy. The product of choice is *Bacillus thuringiensis*, a bacterium that attacks caterpillars only and goes under the name of Dipel, BT or Thuricide. You can also spread granular (also come as liquids) diazinon, Dursban or Sevin and water lightly, about ⅛ inch. And, often, no need to treat your whole lawn—just spot treat damaged areas plus about a 10-foot buffer zone.

FERTILIZERS

The numbers on the bag show the percentages of nitrogen, phosphorus and potassium (in that order) in the fertilizer. Multiply the weight of the bag by each percentage, and you know exactly how many pounds of each nutrient you have. A 50-pound bag of 16-4-8, for instance, contains eight pounds of nitrogen—enough for 8000 square feet of lawn at the usual one-pound-per-1000-square-feet application. A 40-pound bag contains 6.4 (40 lbs. × 16 percent) pounds of nitrogen—enough for 6400 square feet of lawn.

You read a good deal about slow release fertilizers for our Florida sandy soils, especially nitrogen. Urea nitrogen doesn't leach out quite as quickly as nitrate and amoniacal nitrogen, and sulfur coated urea is a bit better still. But neither can be considered slow release. "Natural organic nitrogen" as in manure or sludge is the only true slow release.

Plants take in carbon, hydrogen and oxygen from the air and water. The primary soil/fertilizer nutrients are nitrogen (principally for vegetative, foliar growth), phosphorous (roots, blooms) and potassium (general vigor, hardiness, seed development). Secondary nutrients are sulfur (does all kinds of things), magnesium (chlorophyll) and calcium (cell walls, vigor). Micronutrients are iron, manganese, boron, chlorine, zinc, copper and molybdenum.

You often hear people refer to fertilizer as food. I once heard a county agent warn against this. Plants feed on the carbohydrates they manufacture by photosynthesis. Fertilizers are nutrient stimulants which help plants function better to produce what both you and the plant want it to. Enough fertilizer is enough—and more is less good.

FIGS

The two recommended varieties are Celeste and Brown Turkey.

Celeste (also called Celestial, Blue Celeste, Little Brown and

Sugar) has small, purplish-bronze to light brown fruit with (this is an advantage) a closed eye. The eye is at the top of the fig, and an open one invites water and insects. Celeste ripens mid-July to mid-August, but bears no fruit after a severe winter freeze.

Brown Turkey (Everbearing, Harrison, Ramsey, Lee's Perpetual, Eastern Brown Turkey, Brunswick) has moderate size bronze fruit with a medium eye opening. It ripens late July to late fall, and will fruit following severe freeze damage.

A variety known as Green Ischia is not widely grown, but has the desirable qualities of having green fruit (birds prefer darker fruit) and a closed eye.

These varieties do not need cross-pollination to set fruit. Plant bareroot figs in late winter, container-grown in early spring. Prune to maintain desired size and shape, and head back to promote branching. Wait until regrowth starts to prune freeze-damaged wood.

Figs like lots of water during the fruiting season, and ditto small, monthly fertilizings with 6-6-6 or similar.

Birds will probably be your biggest pest problem; try picking ripe fruit early in the morning. Rusty brown leaves suggest fig rust; spray with Bordeaux mixture or zeneb.

One last thing: Figs produce an enzyme that can cause dermatitis, so gloves are advisable when working with or harvesting figs.

FIRETHORN

Or pyracantha. Evergreen, grows up to 20 feet in a helterskelter manner, is often espaliered. Clusters of white flowers in spring turn into orange-red berries which attract, especially, mocking birds. A rapid, almost lusty grower. A pair of loppers comes in handy, and keep an eye out for lacebugs.

FLEAS

Here in Florida, up to five different kinds of fleas have been found on one animal. We have cat fleas (the most common), dog fleas, human fleas, sticktight fleas and common fleas. Sand fleas are common fleas who live and breed outdoors. Flea eggs hatch into wiry, ⅜ inch white worms which spin tiny cocoons from which adults emerge as full-blown fleas.

Fleas can stay in the cocoon stage for up to five weeks, and adults can live for long periods without feeding. But they get ravenous, and when blood approaches—pet or human—the vibrations signal the cocoons to hatch and the adults to attack—which is why, when you go into a house that's been empty for a while, it sometimes seems suddenly alive with fleas.

Many people don't react to flea bites; others suffer severe allergic reactions; most are in between. The usual bite has a small red dot where the mouth parts entered, a red halo and very little swelling. Fleas have been known to carry plague, typhus and tularemia.

The keys to flea control are 1) treat your pet, 2) treat where it goes, indoors and out, and 3) avoid reinfestation.

Flea collars are helpful, but can't do the job alone.

Your vet can prescribe a product called Proban, which is effective provided pets are kept indoors and additional controls are used in your house and yard.

Frequent combing, shampooing and just plain picking fleas off by hand can do a surprisingly good job of reducing flea infestations.

You can dust your pet with 5% Sevin or spray with a pyrethrin-containing insecticide—best done outdoors over paper so you can spot and kill any fleas that jump off.

Torus and Precor are good indoor insecticides which prevent fleas from becoming adults and have residual effects of up to three months. You can also spray with Dursban, Baygon or pyrethrins.

After vacuuming where fleas may be present, it's good practice to discard the dust bag—and with it any fleas or flea eggs that may have been vacuumed up.

Outdoors, malathion, Dursban, diazinon, Baygon and Sevin are all effective.

GARDENIAS

Selecting the right gardenia for a given situation can be tricky. First off, grafted (onto *Gardenia thunbergia* rootstock) plants are more vigorous and more nematode resistant—but they're not completely winter-hardy north of Tampa-Orlando-Cocoa, where you should stick to own-root plants. Some varieties have large flowers, others small ones. Bloom time varies from early spring to late spring to early summer to all summer long to late August. Shapes and foliage color vary, too. Probably best to talk with a knowing, local nursery before plunging.

You can use gardenias as a shrub border or foundation planting, but they probably do best as free-standing specimens since they don't particularly like to be around other plants. Soil pH should be kept near 6, soil should be amended with two inches of peat moss, leafmold or compost worked in to a depth of six to eight inches. Use a 6-6-6 or 8-8-8 four times a year—spring, summer, fall, winter—but go easy on the minor elements, which can be toxic to gardenias at relatively low concentrations—twice a year is ideal. The usual cause of yellowing leaves is iron deficiency—the treatment, iron sulfate at the rate of about half an ounce per gallon of water.

Prune gardenias just after blooming, but not after October 1st if you want maximum flowers next year. Water is important to bloom, too. Not enough, and buds will drop (a problem with gardenias) before opening; keep the soil evenly moist while plants are in bud.

Probably the most serious disease (fortunately, not too common in Florida) is stem canker—roughened, cracked

areas near the soil line form cankerous growths. No cure—
infected plants should be destroyed. Sooty mold turns leaves
black but does no lasting harm. Scales, aphids, spider mites,
thrips and whitefly can all cause problems.

A fairly high-maintenance plant—but, Oh so worth it.

GERANIUMS

Geraniums are tricky in north and central Florida. Plant them
too early and they run the risk of frost. Plant them later, and
they'll run into summer heat that retards growth and flowering. I tried a row along the front walk, and they all died by July.

The best geraniums I've seen have been in planters or
planted near the house, where they get some relief from the
sun. Best time to try them is when they show up in a local
nursery.

GERBERA DAISY

You may have seen this beguiling South African transplant (it's
also called the Transvaal daisy) in patio pots up north. Down
here, it's hardy to 30° with protection, and will overwinter
provided no prolonged freeze.

The flowers can be spectacular—up to seven inches across;
various shades of red, yellow, pink, orange and scarlet, often
with contrasting eyes; single, double, crested double, full
crested double and something called quilled full crested
double. Gerberas come in so many variations you're probably
better off buying larger, blooming plants so you can see
exactly what you're getting. If you buy smaller plants, plant
them right away—most small-pot gerberas come rootbound
and you'll want to untangle the roots as soon as possible.
Gerberas welcome peat moss and three pounds of 6-6-6 or

8-8-8 per 100 square feet of bed once a month during the growing season. Divide every two years and plant with the crown at ground level. Leaf miners, caterpillars, thrips and mites are their major pest problems.

GLADIOLUS

Gladiolus can be a bit of work, but can also be well worth it.

You can plant the corms up to three months before frost, and you can plant them continuously for continuous blooming (just be sure to store them in peat or something, so they won't dry out). Recommended depth is three inches, though I find if you plant them deeper they're better able to resist the wind, though they'll likely need staking in any event. Add peat or compost, and a shot of bonemeal is always welcome. The books say lift and store corms when foliage has turned brown; last year I planted in the spring and left in the ground after cutting off the dead foliage—and got spectacular late-fall flowers.

Gladioli are subject to thrips, caterpillers, foliage disease and corm-rot—but you're likely to be spraying anyway, so why not add gladioli to your list.

GOLDEN RAIN TREE

A 30 to 35 foot tree that gives welcome color through most of the year, but (especially) large sprays of bright yellow flowers in the fall that give way to attractive orange-red seed pods that last into the new year. Likes well drained soil and a warm climate, but puts up with a wide variety of conditions. Scales are the major pest.

GOPHERS—SEE POCKET GOPHERS

GRAPES

Here in Florida, you have your choice of two basically different types of grapes: The bunch grapes you're used to (though not the same varieties) and muscadine grapes. Muscadines produce single grapes with somewhat thicker skins (but still real good eating), have smaller leaves and fruit, and are either bronze or black. Muscadines have the virtue of being native to Florida: they're seldomly seriously bothered by disease and insects.

Recommended bunch varieties are: Conquistador (similar to Concord, but better) for eating, juice and jelly; Orlando Seedless for the table; and, if you want to make white wine, Stover, Suwannee and Blanc Du Bois.

Muscadine varieties are Triumph and Dixie (bronze) and Southland and Cowart (black) for general purpose use; and Noble (black) for juice and jelly. All of these, both bunch and muscadine, are self-pollenating—no need for male and female vines.

Best planting time is February in central and March in northern Florida. Container grown grapes can be planted anytime.

On two-wire trellises, the wires are usually 2 ½ and 5 feet high; on three-wire trellises, 2, 4 and 6 feet. Set stakes next to each vine and tie to the top wire. As shoots appear, tie the best-looking to the stake and prune off the others. When your main stem reaches the top wire, pinch or cut so that laterals will grow. Keep tying the main stem as it grows, and cut off all laterals except those along the wires.

To prune muscadines, let laterals keep growing out, but prune all shoots from them to six or eight inches. Also, prune all wood less than ¼ inch in diameter. If it looks as if you've pruned too much, you've probably done it just right. Pruning time is January/February in central, and January/mid-March in north Florida.

With bunch grapes, prune everything (except trunk and main laterals) older than one year. Shorten remaining canes to eight or so buds and retie to the trellis.

Keep weeds and grass at least two feet from the vines. Fertilize with ¼ pound of 6-6-6 or 8-8-8 a foot or so away from the stem soon after the first growth begins on new vines—and repeat in May, July and early September. On second year vines, increase the dose to ⅔ of a pound and apply in late March, May and just after harvest. Give new plants an inch to an inch and a half of water at least once every two weeks in April and May—and also during dry spells.

Spray with malathion or Sevin as needed (see your county agent about diseases such as rot) and you'll be picking grapes in August/September for years to come.

GROUND COVERS

Kind of a limited choice. I have a near-by friend who says his pachysandra does fine—but I haven't seen any anywhere else. We have some Blue Pacific Juniper which keeps low and spreads very nicely, if a bit slowly. Other ground covers to consider are other junipers, dwarf jasmine, ivy, liriope, mondo grass and asparagus fern.

HACKBERRY

Another native to north and central Florida. Member of the elm family. 60 to 80 feet with a very straight trunk with very smooth (usually beech-gray) bark with lots of prominent warts. Deciduous. Small orange-to-yellow fruits attract wildlife. Does best on moist, fertile soil, though widely used as a street tree in the middle west. No serious pests.

HEATHER

Not the *Erica* heather of Europe, but a woody shrub called Alysson heather that's loaded with small purple/blue (also a white variety) flowers and bees—lots of bees—right up until frost, at which point they die back, but then come back next spring bigger and better than ever. Makes a nice addition to the foundation or screen room planting, but sooner or later you'll have to prune them back. Perhaps *the* plant to plant if you want bees in your garden.

HERBS

Herbs are very forgiving—most of them will grow anywhere with minimum care, including here. They tend to propagate easily, but unless you enjoy that sort of thing it's easier and quicker to buy them potted, especially at local fairs. Annuals such as basil and dill are easy from seed. Many herbs take well to container growing, including hanging baskets.

A basic herb collection might include basil and dill, parsley (a biennial, grows like crazy here), and perennials such as chives, garlic chives, lemon verbena, pineapple sage and Mexican tarragon—to name just a few of the many there are to choose from.

Normally, herbs are at their aromatic best just before flowering. The old method was to cut the plants, tie the stems together and hang them up somewhere well ventilated to dry. Quicker and less dust-collecting is to pluck the leaves and dry them on a screen propped up so air can circulate under it. Better yet is to pluck the leaves, wash and freeze them. Frozen herbs are easy to crumble into salads, salad dressings, over fish just out of the broiler or oven and still hot—or wherever you want them.

HERBICIDES

Vegetable gardens and flower beds are best weed-controlled by hand, plus hoes and mulch—or, if you're just starting out, a non-selective kill-'em-all such as Roundup or Kleenup.

Lawns are far more difficult. There are a number of preemergence herbicides you can use to keep weed seeds from germinating. Rule of thumb is to apply them mid-February in central and March 1 in north Florida.

Most of the broadleaf postemergence herbicides are based on 2,4-D plus dicambra, sold under many trade names. Normally, the younger the weed seedling, the easier it is to control it, so let that be your application-time guideline. For grass-like weeds such as the sedges and sandburs, you can try Basagran or Image.

In all cases, make sure you read the label completely and follow directions to the letter. A little too much herbicide can seriously damage (or worse) the very lawn you're trying to enhance. Some products (Image and those containing atrazine, for instance) work fine on St. Augustine but can kill bahia.

Proceed with caution.

HIBISCUS

Probably southern Florida's most widely grown plant, but can't take cold—28° to 30° will freeze it to the ground unless well protected.

Mostly one-day, but continuous, flowers in red, orange, yellow, white, lavender and brown, with lots of stops in between. Plants can be low and spreading, tall and upright, compact or open—your county agent can help you select the varieties you want. Best planted in cooler weather. Same depth as in the container. Dig the hole six inches larger in all directions than the root ball. Mix ⅓ peat or compost with the hole soil. Water thoroughly and mulch. May need staking. Fertilize light and often—a small handful to a pound or two (depending on size) of 6-6-6 in early spring, after the first flush of growth, mid-summer and early winter. Manganese (as manganese sulfate, one or two ounces per plant, or as foliar spray), iron and other micronutrients are important.

Hibiscus blooms on new wood. If you suffered winter dieback, prune to the ground in spring and hope for the best. If no damage, prune to desired height and shape in three stages—the longest third of the branches in February or March, the next third in 30 days, and the rest 30 days after that.

Hibiscus attracts a number of sucking and chewing pests;

best to control them with a systemic (Cygon, Orthene) since hibiscus can be sensitive to pesticides.

A nearby nurseryman has hibiscus blooming in his nursery from spring to fall, while the hibiscus around his house doesn't start blooming until July or August. His solution: Replace the old ones with new ones each spring, as you would with an annual—or grow them in tubs or pots you can stick in the garage when a cold snap is due.

HOLLIES

Hollies are a very large group (over 500 cultivated varieties) with lots of uses here in Florida—from accent or specimen plants to formal or informal hedges to dwarf foundation planting. They are mostly evergreen and come male and female (the females have the berries); bees do most of the pollenating from distances up to two miles, so you don't have to worry about it.

Hollies prefer partial shade, but most of them will take full sun. They like rich, well drained, slightly acidic soil. Best planting time is November to March, but you can plant container plants any time. The hole should be a foot wider and six inches deeper than the root ball, and the holly should be at the same depth it was before. You'll want to water during extended dry spells, and fertilize in March and September with one cup of 6-6-6 or 8-8-8 for plants with stems/trunks an inch in diameter or less, and two cups for larger plants—from inside the drip line to about a foot beyond it. The only pruning needed should be to remove dead or diseased branches, to shape or train the plant, and perhaps to maintain a single leader in a specimen plant.

Pests and diseases are seldom a major concern with hollies.

You'll want to keep an eye out for scales, leaf miners, mites and twig dieback.

Once you know what sort of plant you want and what you want it to do, your county agent or a knowing nurseryman can show you how a holly might well fill the bill.

HOLLYHOCKS

Most of the books and charts say they do fine here, but you hardly ever see any, and I've had extremely mixed results with mine.

I planted seed in my original sand bed and got a few small plants which I transplanted into the top soil when it arrived. That was early November. Next summer, one of the plants took off, grew to about eight feet, was loaded with pale pink double blooms and produced a ring of six-foot side shoots also loaded with blooms. People, even northerners, would ask what kind of plant is that.

After that, the best I could do hollyhockwise was about two feet high with a few scrawny flowers—but then, I never had much luck with hollyhocks in Connecticut, either. I think best procedure is to plant seed in the fall, hope they don't come up until February or so, and keep your fingers crossed.

IMPATIENS

Just as useful here as up north for borders, planters and hanging baskets—until frost gets them. Pinch the main stem for stockier, bushier plants. For shade only until the New

Guinea and other more sun-tolerant varieties came along. Aphids and caterpillars the two main pests.

INDIAN HAWTHORN

Known to the purists by its Latin name, *Raphiolepis*. An evergreen, globish-shaped shrub ranging from dwarf to about five feet. The pink-blooming variety is subject to fungal disease; the white-flowered has almost no problems. A common and altogether useful plant in the home landscape.

INSECT AND RELATED PEST CONTROL

In a nutshell, we have two kinds of insecticides, five main groups of insects and a newly developing philosophy on how to control them.

The insecticides are topical, which work on the surface of the plant, and systemic, which are absorbed by the plant and work from the inside.

The philosophy is, the fewer poisons, the better. Use soap on soft-bodied insects—it erodes the cuticle layer and the insect dehydrates. Use the bacterium *Bacillus thuringiensis* (sold as Dipel, BT or Thuricide) on caterpillars—it kills caterpillars only, has no effect on birds, pets, people or even other insects. Use oil sprays (more heat-resistant ones are on the way) on scale insects. And learn to recognize and encourage beneficial insects.

Now for the five main groups of insect pests (most of what follows applies to woody shrubs, ornamentals, turf and flowers—for vegetables and fruits, always be guided by product labels):

1. Sucking Pests which suck the juices out of plants rather than chew at them.

Scales and mealybugs. When new spring growth starts to harden, use an oil spray such as Volck, or even more effective Volck oil plus malathion—see Volck label for directions. When the temperature goes over 80°F, you'll probably be better off with a systemic such as Cygon, which has the additional advantage of not harming natural scale parasites.

Aphids and whiteflies. Use Safer Insecticidal Soap (or two tablespoons of liquid hand dishwashing detergent per gallon of water), diazinon, malathion—or a systemic such as Cygon or Orthene.

Lacebugs. Topical malathion or Sevin, systemic Cygon or Orthene are all effective, with a second application in 10 to 14 days.

Thrips. Malathion, Cygon or Orthene, with a second application in 7 to 10 days.

2. Chewing Pests.

Caterpillars, webworms and other things that hatch from moth and butterfly eggs. You can use malathion or Sevin, but I've been using Thuricide exclusively and have yet to find a resistant caterpillar.

Grasshoppers, katydids. Diazinon.

Beetles. Diazinon or Sevin.

3. Spider Mites. One of Florida's commonest pests, and can flatten a shrub practically overnight. Not an insect, but related to the spiders. Very small and hard to detect unless you shake them onto a piece of white paper or see tiny webs. Do their damage by sucking plant juices and chlorophyll. Control them with soap solution, Volck oil or Volck oil plus malathion.

4. Leaf Miners. These are the larvae of small flies, moths or beetles. They burrow between the leaf surfaces and leave those zig-zag white trails you often see on (for instance) tomato plants. Some miners leave blotches instead of trails. All miners are hard to get at, and you almost have to use a systemic such as Cygon or Orthene. Of the non-systemics, diazinon offers the best (though limited) control. Fortunately, leaf miner damage is seldom severe.

5. Borers. Mostly the larvae of a moth or a beetle, and they come in three main groups: Pine borers who bore in the inner bark and dine on the cambium layer. Twig borers who bore into small limbs and twigs. And just plain old borers who bore deep into the trunk

Generally, borers prefer trees that have been previously injured and thus weakened, so keeping your trees healthy and free from stress is the best control. If you see signs that borers are present, use lindane or Dursban according to directions.

6. Odds and Ends.

Sooty mold. A black fungus that grows on the excretions (called honeydew) of aphids, mealybugs, many soft scales and (especially) whiteflies. It doesn't look nice, but it doesn't do any real harm. Control the bugs and you'll control the mold. You can also wash it off with soapy water.

Ants. They like honeydew, too, and sometimes actually move aphids from one plant to another that suits them better. Diazinon, Dursban or Sevin, or Amdro bait, directed at the nest, offer effective control.

Millepedes (those hard-bodied things that often roll up into a ball), *pillbugs and sowbugs* (both about half an inch long, oval, gray to brown with seven pairs of legs). Repeated applications of diazinon or Sevin if you have a problem with these.

Slugs (without shells) and *snails* (with shells). Mesurol bait or Metaldehyde dust, spray or bait. I know, lots of people use a plate of beer to good effect. I've tried that in four different states, and have still to see it work.

JASMINE

A fragrant vine for full sun to partial shade—or if you wish you can trim it as a shrub. Confederate jasmine is the white one,

Carolina the yellow. Semi-evergreen and easy to grow—you often see it on fences and stumps along the roadside.

JERUSALEM THORN

Member of the pea family. An attractive, fast growing, small (20 to 25 feet), spreading tree with feathery foliage and bright yellow flowers. Native to Texas and the southwest. Deciduous. Leaves are long and slender; thorns up to an inch long can be a nuisance. May need occasional pruning. Can be rooted from cuttings. Drought resistant, grows on most well-drained soils, including light sand. Pests include caterpillars, scales and twig dieback.

LACE BUGS

Up to a third of an inch long, boxy-rectangular shape, with lacy wings that extend beyond the body. Especially fond of pyracantha, azaleas, oaks, sycamores and elms. They come in droves, suck leaf juices to produce lackluster foliage, and deposit a silvery residue that eventually turns brown. Malathion and the systemics Cygon and Orthene are all effective, with a follow-up application in 10 to 14 days.

LARVA

The eggs of moths, beetles and flies hatch worm-like young known as larvae—more specifically, caterpillars, grubs and maggots. This is the form that does the damage—eating away at your plants, molting as they grow bigger, then finally transforming into an inactive stage (the pupa, cocoon or chrysalis) from which it emerges as a full-grown insect. Contrast this with nymphs.

LAWN CARE

Since Bermuda, carpet and zoysia are so little used (you can always get information from your County Agent), we'll limit this to the routine maintenance—watering, fertilizing and cutting—of bahia, centipede and St. Augustine.

The preferred way to water is on an "as needed" basis—the catch being that when watering is needed, it's needed now and not two days from now. When grass turns grayish-blue and/or wilts, 3/4 of an inch of water is in order, which comes to 465 gallons per 1000 square feet. If you water on a set schedule, aim at 3/4 of an inch per week, with allowance for rain. Grass doesn't need any more water than that, and in fact more than that can invite disease and other problems. Best time to water is early morning when grass can dry quickly. Worst time is late afternoon/early evening when grass may remain moist (and inviting) much of the night.

With fertilizing, you can take your pick of a high level, low level or in-between maintenance program. Bahia high level: 16-4-8 in March and early September; iron in April and October; and high nitrogen (30-0-0) in May and July. Centipede high level: 16-4-8 in March and August; iron April and July; high nitrogen in June. St. Augustine high level: 16-4-8 in March and September; iron in June; high nitrogen in May and July. For low level maintenance, skip the high nitrogen. For in between, skip one of the high nitrogens. A 10-10-10 instead of 16-4-8 in the fall is perfectly ok.

The coverage you're aiming at with the 16-4-8 and high nitrogen is one pound of nitrogen per 1000 square feet.

Multiply the percentage of nitrogen by the weight of the bag to find out how many pounds of nitrogen you have. Always try to water in fertilizer as soon as possible. Recommended iron dose is two ounces of iron sulfate in three to five gallons of water per 1000 square feet of lawn, or a chelated iron according to the label. In a low maintenance program, iron is indicated whenever grass turns yellow. When bahia gets $4\frac{1}{2}$ to 6 inches high, cut it back to 3 to 4 inches. Ditto low and moderate level St. Augustine. In high level St. Augustine, cut 3 inch blades back to 2 inches. Keep centipede cut to $1\frac{1}{2}$ to 2 inches. Try not to cut off more than one third at a time. And don't collect the clippings. They'll add up to about one extra fertilizing per year—of the best slow-release sort—and they don't contribute to thatch build-up.

LEAF DIAGNOSIS

No guarantees go with this, but nutritional deficiencies tend to cause specific symptoms in foliage, and what follows may be useful (if not definitive) in coping with plant problems.

Older leaves go first: deficiency, symptoms, remedy.

Nitrogen. Loss of green color, leaves thickened and brittle, plant stunted, foliage sparse. High nitrogen fertilizer.

Potassium. Marginal leaf scorch, marginal leaf tip yellowing, irregular gradual decay, brown palm leaves. Muriate of potash.

Magnesium. Inverted green V, band across the leaves, interveinal yellowing. Quite common. Magnesium sulfate (epsom salts).

Younger leaves first:

Sulfur. Uniform loss of green color. Iron sulfate or liquid iron with sulfur.

Iron. Interveinal yellowing, fine green veins, netted leaf appearance, yellow grass. Iron sulfate or liquid iron.

Manganese. Interveinal yellowing, frizzled sago palm fronds. Manganese sulfate, especially for palms.

Copper. Reduced leaf size, cupping of leaves. Copper sulfate.

Molybdenum. Strapped leaves, prominent veination.

Boron. Corky raised areas on leaf underside, tip dieback. Infrequent. Boraxo.

Zinc. Interveinal yellowing with large wavy margins.

Calcium. Yellowing, thickened brittle leaves, short clubby roots. Calcium chloride. Uncommon in Florida soils.

Phosphorous. Reduced leaf size, dull cast. Both new and old leaves. Super phosphate.

LETTUCE

A cool-season crop, best planted in September or October. You see Great Lakes and Buttercrunch seeds in most of the garden stores—but I've had infinitely better luck with romaine.

LICHENS

Greyish/greenish growths that look like scales or scabs on the trunks and branches of trees.

Botanically, lichens are algae and fungi living together in symbiosis. The fungi provide the algae with a safe, secure place to live, and the algae provide the fungi with nutrients via photosynthesis.

Lichens may look a little unsightly, but they cause no known harm to their host trees. If you don't like them, you can scrape them off with a not-too-stiff wire brush or spray them with copper sulfate.

LIGUSTRUM

In Connecticut, privet was privet and that was pretty much that. Down here, privet is called ligustrum, it comes in many foliages, shapes and sizes and is one of our most important hedges/ornamental shrubs/small trees.

Ligustrums are low-cost, readily available, grow rapidly, adapt to most soils and habitats and tolerate full sun to partial shade, extreme cold, heavy pruning and benign neglect. They grow too fast for low-maintenance foundation planting, but by the same token, and because they withstand severe pruning, they make super hedges, accent shrubs, specimen and patio trees.

Established plants should be fertilized two to four times a year—early spring, mid-summer, with optional late spring and early winter—with half a cup to a cup of 6-6-6 or 8-8-8 per plant.

For aphids, scales, whiteflies and spider mites, see Insect Control. For sooty mold, either ignore or wash with soapy water. For leaf spot, destroy infected leaves and try Daconil 2787.

LOBLOLLY BAY

Related to camellias and the commercial tea plant. 40 to 50 feet, evergreen, native to north and central Florida. Leaves look a little like small magnolia leaves, and the flowers (up to 3½ inches) also resemble magnolias. Semi-shade or full sun, ideally on wet soil. You often see stands of them growing alongside the road. No serious pests.

LOQUATS

If you live in north Florida, the loquat makes a 25-foot specimen tree with dark green 8-to-10-inch leaves, very fragrant white flower panicles and cold hardiness down to 10° F.

If you live where the temperature stays above 27°, you get all this plus about 100 pounds of tart to sweet (depends on the variety) 1-to-2 inch oval fruits that are excellent eaten fresh or frozen and make superior jams, jellies, preserves and pies—just be sure to let fruit ripen on the tree.

Loquats bloom in late fall or winter and produce fruit about four months later. Almost any well drained, salt-free soil will do. Although loquats tolerate drought, some irrigation is advisable during bloom and fruit development. Loquats are not fussy eaters, but some fertilizer is necessary for good fruit production; something along the order of 8-4-8 with 3 to 4 percent magnesium will give good results.

No pruning is necessary except for the occasional removal of dead wood. Fruit size and quality can be improved by pruning branches so that fewer clusters of fruit are produced and remaining clusters are exposed to the sun.

LOVEBUGS

If you're new to Florida, come next April-May or August-September you have an unwelcome discovery ahead of you. That's when the lovebugs show up—by the millions. Black, with a dot of red. Females ⅓ inch, males ¼. They won't do you any harm, but they can sure make a mess of your car, splattering into your grill, radiator and windshield. A screen to cover the grill is definitely in order, and the sooner you wash off dead lovebugs, the less the chance of damage to your paint.

Lovebugs were first reported in Florida in Escambia County in 1947. They showed up in Leon County in 1955–56, and in Alachua and Marion Counties in 1964–65. In recent years, they seem to have subsided a bit in north central Florida.

There's not much point in spraying lovebugs—there are just too many of them. But if you're driving, try to do it at night or early morning. Lovebugs spend the night on low-growing vegetation, and generally don't get up until around 10:00 AM.

MAGNOLIA

The southern magnolia, as distinct from the Japanese magnolia that blooms so early up north (here, too, increasingly). Native to north and central Florida. Gets up to 80 feet tall, rather slowly. A large, upright-spreading evergreen that provides dense shade, large, creamy-white, fragrant blooms—and an almost endless supply of big, tough fallen leaves. Does best in fertile, well-drained soil, shade or full sun—but in truth you see them growing almost everywhere. Pests include scale and twig borer.

MAPLE, Red

A native tree, and the only maple you see here—at least, that I've seen here—although others are shown as growing here and one is even called the Florida maple. Provides welcome summer shade and equally welcome yellow and red fall foliage. Similar to, if not identical with, what we used to call swamp or rock maple. Up to 60 feet tall. Prefers good soil and moist locations. A beautiful tree that should be more widely planted—provided you have moist soil or are prepared to do a lot of watering. Sensitive to wounding; look carefully before you buy, and mulch to keep the weed eater away (and to hold in moisture).

MARIGOLD

One of the most heat resistant summer flowers, and the one you see everywhere. The tall ones often need staking; the short ones fend for themselves. Plant them March 15 through May in the north, March through August in central. Cut off dead flowers, and you should have flowers for three or four months.

MEALYBUGS

See Scale Insects and Mealybugs.

MOLE CRICKETS

Ugly-looking things an inch to 1½ inches long. Resembles a thin cricket with stubby forelegs good for digging.

Mole crickets prefer bahiagrass, but you'll also find them in St. Augustine and Bermudagrass. They tunnel through the soil near the surface looking for organic matter (including grass roots) and small insects to eat. Doing this can uproot grass and cause it to dry out and die. Unchecked, mole crickets can turn turf into bare soil. They feed at night during warm weather, especially after rain or irrigation, then retreat to their permanent burrows and stay there until the weather suits them again.

You can easily spot mole crickets by the fist-size mounds of sand they push up from their tunneling. If you want to find out just how bad your infestation is, mix 1½ ounces of hand dishwashing detergent in two gallons of water and sprinkle over several locations that add up to four square feet. If you see three or more mole crickets emerge within three minutes, you have a problem.

You can help solve it with sprays, granules or baits containing diazinon or Dursban. Pick a night when the temperature will be 60° or more. Water your lawn beforehand if using a bait, afterwards if using a spray or granules. Best time is probably mid-June when mole crickets are at the height of their hatching and emerging season.

MISTLETOE

Those bright green orbs you see up in the trees—especially the laurel oaks in winter—are mistletoe. Unlike Spanish moss and lichens, mistletoe is a parasite. It photosynthizes its own food, using water and nutrients it takes from its host.

MOLES

A small (4½ to 6½ inches, not counting his stubby tail) mammal with oversize, spade-like feet for digging. Has an insatiable appetite for grubs, worms and other good things that live in the soil. Active day and night in burrows just below the surface—but also have deeper, permanent tunnels that include a nest (the young are born in March). Moles prefer moist, sandy-loam soils, and don't like dry soils at all. They can make a mess of your lawn (even while de-grubbing and aerating it) and getting rid of them is no easy task. Poisons and repellents are next to useless. Most garden stores sell traps—tamp down a section of the burrow; if it's repaired in a couple of hours, it's an active run and that's where you put your trap. Another way to discourage them is to kill off their food with diazinon, Dursban or Sevin.

MULBERRY

Often called Red Mulberry. A deciduous, very fast growing (up to 50 feet) native tree whose edible berries (look like anemic blackberries) attract all kinds of wildlife, but make an unholy mess when they start to turn black and fall. Does best in full sun on fertile soil, but will grow in a variety of situations. Has no serious pest problems. Related to the figs.

MUSHROOM ROOT ROT

In the fall you may see large clumps of fairly large (though this varies) honeyish-colored mushrooms growing on stumps or around the base of shrubs and trees, especially oaks. These are honey mushrooms, one of the few mushrooms that feed on living wood—or, more precisely, living roots. The main part of the mushroom is called the mycellium, similar to (but much larger than) the fuzz on the grape jelly in the back of the refrigerator. This mycellium feeds on the roots, making them easily peeled and slimy, and eventually kills the plant. There's not much you can do except dig up the plant (assuming it's diggable), discard it and fumigate the nearby soil—assuming a product like Vapam is still on the market.

The honey mushroom, incidentally, is closely related to those giant mushroom systems recently reported from Michigan-Wisconsin and the northeast Pacific coast.

MUSTARD

Grown for the greens. September-May north, September-March central. An excellent candidate for wide-row planting. Southern Giant Curled and Florida Broad Leaf are favorite varieties.

NANDINA

Also called heavenly bamboo, though it isn't a bamboo at all. A very useful, slow growing, 6 to 8-foot evergreen with bright red berries in fall and winter. Not fussy about soil, and all but trouble-free.

NARCISSUS

Or paperwhite. Sometimes called Narcissus Tazetta. By whatever name, as close as you're going to come to the perennial spring daffodils here in Florida. Plant bulbs September through December, eight inches apart, four inches deep—or a little deeper if you want to naturalize them with minimum lifting and separating—or a little shallower if you want quick split-up into bulblet offshoots. Full sun to partial shade, and go easy on soil amendments and fertilizer, although a little bone meal will be welcome.

With a little luck, you can (in a manner of speaking) eat your paperwhites and have them, too. Several neighbors have forced the bulbs for Christmas, then planted them in the garden with good results.

NECTARINES—SEE PEACHES

NEMATODES

Your snapdragons are doing well, except for those in the middle and over there. Parts of your lawn don't seem to respond to fertilizing, or even to watering. A chrysanthemum suddenly starts to go limp. You just gave that plant iron, but its leaves keep turning yellow anyway. Those two tomatoes keep dropping their fruit—the others produce beautifully. Didn't this shrub used to put out bigger leaves, and more of them?

Could be a number of things, including nematodes—tiny ($1/100$th to $1/8$th inch), skinny, colorless, very hard-to-see worms with needle-like beaks who live in soil moisture and plant tissue, feed on plant cells and occur erratically.

A root examination shows galls or knots—often with swelling at the tips—or not many feeder roots—or darker color than usual—or signs of root decay.

A soil and root analysis—you can get a Nematode Sample Kit from your county agent, cost $8—confirms that you do indeed have nematodes. And, with one exception, there's not much you can do about it except call in a qualified pest control operator, destroy the affected area and start again.

That exception is a bed you use for vegetables or flowers. Come June or July, when the sun is hot and the days are long, till to a depth of six inches, rake as smooth as you can, water thoroughly and let sit for one to three days. Then cover with clear, not black, plastic, seal all edges and seams with soil, and let bake for six weeks. Soil surface should heat up to 120° F or more—enough to kill not only nematodes, but also other pests and disease organisms. The better the contact between the clear plastic and the soil, the better your results will be. And don't till when you take up the plastic—just plant as usual.

There are a number of things you can do to make life not so easy for nematodes. Don't plant members of the same family (tomatoes, peppers, potatoes, eggplant, for instance) where one of them grew last year—and don't follow a root crop with another root crop, regardless of the family. When a plant stops producing, pull it before its roots play host to another generation of nematodes. The more organic matter in your soil, the less damage nematodes seem to do. When there's a choice, plant resistant varieties—your county agent can help you with this. Fabric root barriers tend to retard or delay recontamination from adjoining areas. And well-maintained plants can withstand nematodes (and everything else, for that matter) better than plants under stress.

NICOTIANA

An old favorite, the tobacco plant. Plant seeds from March 15 on and enjoy flowers and fragrance through August or even September. I prefer the white to the colored flowers.

NYMPHS

A nymph is an immature insect born looking like its parent, except no wings. Plant bugs such as aphids, scales and whiteflies, also leafhoppers, grasshoppers and thrips all produce nymphs—which start eating your vegetation as soon as they're born, and molt periodically as they increase in size.

The other immature insect form is larva, which see.

OAK, Laurel

Native to most parts of Florida. Fast growing, 60 to 80 feet. Similar to live oak, except the leaves are smooth, flat, shiny green both top and bottom—and fall off when the weather turns cold. Does well in wide variety of soils. Does best in full sun. Stands up to the wind. Easily maintained. All in all, a beautiful shade tree which should be more widely planted. Pests include caterpillars and mushroom root rot.

OAK, Live

It's hard to fathom why live oaks aren't planted more often. It's not *that* slow a grower, especially when young; it's native; it prefers good soil and moisture, but will take almost anything you give it—and it's certainly the most beautiful and durable of all our oaks. It's also our only evergreen one—not that it doesn't shed leaves (it does the year round), it just doesn't shed them all at once. A wide spread crown up to 50 feet, with almost horizontal limbs. The leaf edges curl under, as opposed to laurel oak leaves, which lie flat. Caterpillars can be a (minor) problem; Dipel or Thuricide is a good solution.

OAK, Shumard

A north Florida native. Large (over 100 feet) member of the red oak group with dense, beautiful green foliage and striking fall color. Medium speed grower. Produces acorns every other year. Does best in rich, fertile soil. An excellent park or specimen tree. Pests include caterpillars and heart rot.

OKRA

Likes hot weather. Plant March-July in north, March-August in central. Clemson Spineless, Perkins, Dwarf Green, Emerald and Blondy are recommended. Susceptible to root-knot nematodes.

OLEANDER

When you live in Ocala, you don't often think of oleander, although it grows here (somewhat). But when you visit, for instance, Sarasota in May, you have (to say the least) another think coming. From short trees to shrubs to dwarf varieties— from white to palest shades of pink to deep reds. Evergreen, and covered with blooms all summer long. Almost as much a must as azaleas a bit further north, and quite a bit easier to grow. Main pest is the oleander caterpillar, which can denude the plant virtually overnight.

ONIONS

Bulbing. September-December both north and central. You may have been used to long-day onion varieties up north; here you'll want short-day varieties such as Excel, Texas Grano, Granex (from which the Vidalia developed), White Granex and Tropicana Red.

Bunching, like scallions. August to March in both regions, whenever plants or sets are available. Recommended varieties are White Portugal, Evergreen, Beltsville Bunching, Perfecto Bianco and Shallots. Multipliers, so-called, are onion plants that don't form a bulb, but continue to produce more plants throughout the growing season. At harvest time, dig them all, replant a few to keep multiplying and use the rest.

PALMS

The key to a successful palm is to get it well established in its first transplant year. That's much easier done with a container grown palm (small and slow growing, with most of its roots intact) than a field grown palm (large, slow growing, and having to grow practically a whole new root system).

You can plant a palm anytime, but June is best to catch the warm, rainy summer months—palms grow slower in cold months, and cold damage is much worse with not-well-established palms. If you have a balled-and-burlaped palm, keep it in the shade, water the root ball daily and get it into the ground as quickly as possible. Dig the hole twice as wide as the root ball and a little bit deeper. Water the root ball when planting to eliminate air pockets. Plant at the same depth as before. Current thinking is don't add soil amendments—they encourage the roots to stay close to home rather than go off seeking different, greener pastures. Mulch heavily. Water daily the first few weeks and frequently thereafter. Apply a foliar nutrient spray every three or four months during the first year. Fertilize several weeks after planting, then every mid-winter, mid-summer and early fall. Some people advocate using a special palm fertilizer. Others prefer a 2-1-1 ratio, a 16-4-8 or a 12-4-8. You can also use an 8-8-8. Whatever you use, make sure it contains minor elements, especially iron, magnesium and manganese. For new palms with no clear trunks, use about two pounds per application. When they get bigger and show a clear trunk, up the dose to about half a pound of 16-4-8 or a pound of 8-8-8 per inch of trunk diameter. After the first year, maintenance should be routine, with a minimum of pest and disease problems. It's normal for lower fronds to turn brown and die—the sooner you cut or saw them off, the easier.

Now for the all-important question, Which palm for your area?

Starting with north Florida, the common palms are

1. The Sabal or Cabbage Palm. Grows 30 to 60 feet. Very adaptable to wet or dry soil conditions. Fan shaped (as opposed to feathery) leaves. The Florida state tree.
2. California Washington Palm. Fan shaped. Well drained soil. Too tall for most home plantings at 50 to 60 feet.
3. European Fan. Two to five feet. Bushy. Tolerates many soils. An excellent, small palm.
4. Needle Palm. Fan. Three to five feet. Fertile, moist soil and shade. Very cold hardy.
5. Pindo Palm. Most cold hardy of the feathery palms. Ten

to 20 feet. Most soils. And you can make jelly out of the fruits. An all-around winner.

6. Windmill. Fan. Most soils. Five to 10 feet. Very cold hardy.

This next group of palms needs to be sited so they get some cold protection, or a little further south.

7. Lady Palm. Fan. Eight to 10 feet. Moist, semi-shaded. An excellent patio or container palm.
8. Chinese Fan. 30 feet. Most soils.
9. Paurotis Palm. Feathery. 10 to 20 feet. Moist, fertile soil.
10. Senegal Date Palm. Feathery. 20 to 25 feet. Well drained.

The following palms will grow in north Florida, but they all have complications, and you hardly ever see them.

11. Canary Island Date Palm. Fan. 30 feet. Adaptable. Too large for most residential plantings, prone to magnesium deficiency.
12. Date Palm. Feathery. 30 to 40 feet. Well drained. Too large, seldom produces fruit in Florida.
13. Dwarf Palmetto. Fan. Three to six feet. Moist. Difficult to transplant.
14. Hispaniolan Palmetto. Fan. 35 to 60 feet. Sandy soil. Large, heavy and seldom available.
15. Mexican Washington Palm. Fan. 60 to 80 feet. Very adaptable. Excellent—if you live in the Taj Mahal.
16. Puerto Rican Hat Palm. Fan. 30 to 40 feet. Sandy. Too large for most homesites.
17. Saw Palmetto. Fan. Three to four feet. Extremely adaptable. An excellent small, native plant—but extremely difficult to transplant.
18. Wild Date Palm. Feathery. 60 to 80 feet. Variable. Seldom available.

You'll notice no mention is made here of the so-called Sago Palm. Actually, this isn't a palm at all, but a cycad—and as such deserves its own write-up.

PAMPAS GRASS

Best used as an isolated clump-specimen or as a screen. Too tall—8 to 20 feet—for foundation planting. Once established (which can take some time) a very low-maintenance plant. 16-4-8 twice a year, no real bug or disease problems, prune away any winter kill, and keep in bounds by chopping root-spread with an axe or spade. Only female plants bear plumes, but most nursery pots contain enough individual shoots to give you both sexes. Spray dried or drying plumes with hair spray or artist's fixative to prevent shedding.

PANSIES

With snapdragons and petunias, the heart of the winter flower garden; in warmer parts, often joined by calendulas. Seasonally available in multi-packs (three or four plants per sectionalized pot) and in bunches of 25. Set out October through February, pinch dead blooms, and pansies will keep flowering through May or June. A difficult plant to grow from seed.

PANTRY PESTS

Common varieties include flour beetles, grain beetles, cigarette beetles, larder beetles, granary weevils, rice weevils, spider beetles, grain moths, flour moths and grain mites—all of which attack stored food and render it unfit to eat.

Best way to avoid these pests is to store food in tightly closed containers—and if you do get an infestation, heat infested food in the oven at 130° F for 30 minutes to kill the pests, and then discard. Keep all storage areas cleaned and vacuumed; you can also apply diazinon, Dursban or Baygon according to directions.

PARSLEY

A three-inch pot of curly parsley costs less than a packet of seed, is surer, and will give you half a dozen or so plants. If they do as well as mine, you'll have all the parsley you (and your neighbors, too) can use for the next 18 months or so. The recommended planting dates are February and March for north, December and January for central, but easier to follow your local garden stores—when they offer parsley, you plant it.

PEAS, English

What we called plain old peas up north. Plant January-March in north Florida, September-March in central. Recommended varieties are Wando, Green Arrow, Laxton's Progress and the edible pod Sugar Snap.

PEAS, Southern

A summer crop, as opposed to English peas. March-August north, March-September central. As with beans, half the usual fertilizer, and no need for inoculated seed. Cowpea curculio is a common pest—ditto a tiny white grub which infests peas in the pod. Recommended are Blackeye, Mississippi Silver, Texas Cream 40, Snapea, Zipper Cream, Sadandy and Purplehull.

PEACHES AND NECTARINES

These two stone fruits are so alike they're treated as one and the same. Other stone fruits—apricots, cherries, almonds and plums—are not well adapted to Florida.

Growth is in three stages: soft pit with little flesh; pit hardens (you can tell when with a penknife); flesh develops rapidly.

They require more care than most homeowners want to give. The two most important considerations are cultivar selection and site selection.

On cultivars, call your county agent to find out how many chilling hours (which see) you get, then pick the cultivar to match. Freestones are preferred over clings for home gardens.

Most important site aspect is to avoid low spots which act as frost pockets—one late season frost can wipe out an entire crop. Good air circulation and water drainage are important. Best pH is 6.0 to 6.5. If you're planting more than one tree, space them about 20 feet apart

Ideal size is 2½ to 4 feet. In sandy soil, plant a little deeper than grown in the nursery. Best planting time is December, so roots can develop before spring growth.

Watering is not critical, but you will want to keep weeds and grass away. In heavy soils, fertilize with an 8-8-8; in sandy soils, a 12-4-8—both with zinc.

Pruning is most important—for shape, and for the amount of fruit. You want an open center so sun can reach all parts of the tree. Best pruning time is January or February, to avoid winter injury. Most peach trees produce far more fruit than they can handle. Much of it will fall off of its own accord when quite small—but that's not enough. When the pit begins to harden, thin to one fruit every six inches.

Fruits don't ripen uniformly—you'll want to check every two days or so.

PEARS

North Florida varieties include Baldwin and Tenn (late blooming) and Flordahome and Hood (early blooming). South of Gainesville to about Orlando, best stick to Hood or to Flordahome (which need cross pollination) and Hood. All four are good both fresh and canned.

Pears do best in sandy loam soil. Best planting time is December/January to give roots time to establish themselves before spring growth begins. Trees planted in late spring may die during the dry periods which often follow.

Prune broken or extra-long roots, and don't let the roots dry out. Dig the hole large enough so roots aren't crowded, bent or broken. Plant at the same depth as at the nursery. Water when hole is about ⅔ full to settle soil around the roots, then finish filling the hole and water again. Do not fertilize at time of planting.

Prune to remove dead wood and for shape—the more open, the better. Fertilize in January and June with 6-6-6 or 8-8-8—about half a pound each time for each year of tree age, up to a level of about five pounds per application. Overfertilizing is bad for pears. Watering may be needed every 7 to 14 days in extremely dry seasons—two inches or more under the entire canopy.

Leaf spot can cause serious defoliation of some varieties; two tablespoons of copper fungicide spray at first bloom, with repeats as needed, should control it. Fire blight can be a serious problem; best call your county agent for advice. For scale, spray with a half cup of 90 percent oil concentrate per gallon of water, ideally in mid-January.

When pears ripen on the tree, they tend to get gritty and sometimes get over-ripe. Best way around this is to pick pears when they've reached full size and are starting to show yellow. Wrap them in paper and keep at room temperature until fully ripe.

PEAT

You'll find two kinds of peat here in Florida—Canadian peat derived from sphagnum moss, and Florida peat, also known as muck. The Canadian variety is probably what you're used to as a water-holding soil amendment and mulch. The Florida variety occurs in pockets throughout the state, but mostly in south Florida where it can be a valuable growing soil, similar to the black dirt in various parts of the country.

PECANS

Pecans make large, beautiful shade trees, but don't count on sending all your friends a box of nuts for Christmas. It can take 8 to 10 years for a pecan to start bearing. You'll be at war with squirrels—estimates are that a single squirrel puts away 54 pounds of pecans a year. And bumper crops are usually followed by tiny ones.

Pecans can grow throughout Florida, but do better from Ocala north. They like well drained soil. Plant December to February. Prune broken and sickly roots, and take pains not to let the roots dry out. Dig your hole 18 to 24 inches wide and two to three feet deep. Spread the roots, and water as you fill. Make a water well and water frequently. Do not fertilize until later. Remove the top third to half of the tree immediately after planting. And if you plant two trees, leave about 60 feet between them—they grow that large.

Keep weeds at least 3 feet from the trunk. Fertilize with 8-8-8 ratio in May, one pound per tree under the canopy—then two pounds for every year the tree is old up to 25 pounds maximum each February. Zinc is very important to pecans; if your fertilizer is low in zinc, add two to four ounces of zinc oxide the first two years, then one pound after that. Water is also very important. Fill the water well every 7 to 10 days during dry spells, and under no circumstances let a young pecan wilt.

Pruning is important, too, to remove dead wood and to force a central leader by cutting off all buds except a dominant one growing upwards. Let side shoots start at five to six feet—ideally three or four spaced around the tree every 12 to 18 inches.

Pecans are too big for easy pest control. Best bet is to rake fallen twigs and leaves and toss them or burn them.

Stuart is probably the most widely planted cultivar in the southeast, but is not recommended for south Florida. Curtis is a superior variety developed in Alachua County. And Elliott is another Florida native originating near Pensacola. There are other good varieties—you might want to call your county agent for his advice.

When you're ready to harvest—October and/or November—you can knock pecans down with a long pole or just let them fall on their own. The sooner you harvest, though, the fewer you'll lose to the squirrels, and the more you'll have to send your friends.

PENTAS

I've never seen a plant attract butterflies the way pentas, especially red ones, do. They're woody perennials that grow

about three feet tall, bloom all summer, thrive on neglect—
and usually come back from the roots in spring. When we
came here in 1988 you hardly ever saw a penta; now they're
deservedly everywhere. Take full sun or shifting shade.
Besides red, come in pink, lavender, blue and white.

PEPPERS

Another two-season crop. Set plants February-April and again
July-August in north Florida, January-March and August- September in central. Do best when mulched. Mosaic virus (not
much you can do about it) is not uncommon. Sweet varieties
are Early Calwonder, Yolo Wonder, Big Bertha, Sweet Banana
and Cubanelle. Hungarian Wax and Jalapeno are recommended
hot varieties. I've had extremely good luck with sweet peppers—they don't get very big, but there are lots of them.

PERIWINKLE

Despite the fact it is killed by frost, you see this impatiens-like
pink and white flower everywhere. Thrives in full sun or
partial shade, and will grow in just about any old Florida soil.
Reseeds itself, but the new generation is never quite up to the
old. Up to two feet in height, with (in extreme cases) a spread
up to five feet. Is sometimes called creeping periwinkle, but
I've yet to see one creep.

PERSIMMONS

The persimmon is a fruit that may be coming into its own—
again. The wild variety that grew from Connecticut to Florida

and as far west as Kansas and Texas was used by both the Indians and early settlers. But the fruit is very small, the seeds very large and the flesh very astringent unless fully ripe.

Oriental persimmon seeds were introduced by Commodore Matthew Perry in 1856—but they froze. In the 1870's, the Department of Agriculture planted grafted, imported trees in the south, but they never quite caught on.

Now there are several varieties well worth considering:

Tanenashi—the most popular persimmon grown in Florida. Fruits are 3″ or more, deep yellow to orange, astringent until ripe, usually seedless—and make a very pretty sight on a loaded tree.

Fuyu—fruits about three inches across, deep reddish color, orange flesh, few seeds and no astringency. You can pick and eat them the way you would an apple, while the flesh is still crisp and firm.

Hanafuyu—another non-astringent variety. Large reddish-orange fruits with excellent flavor, sweet and juicy. Ripens September and October.

Saijo—extremely sweet. Fruits too small for the market, but recommended for the home garden.

There are other good varieties—check with your nurseryman or county agent.

Pollination is usually not a problem with persimmons. Most varieties bear only female flowers which form fruit on their own—usually seedless. When pollination takes place, no more seedless.

Plant bare-root trees in December or January. Take care not to let the roots dry out. You can plant container trees any time, with plenty of water during dry spells.

Prune extra-long or injured roots. Dig the hole big enough to avoid crowding and set at the same depth as at the nursery. Pack soil tightly, make a well around the hole and fill with water.

Mulch two to three feet out from the trunk and allow 15 to 20 feet between trees.

Don't fertilize at planting—wait until April or May. Then use a balanced 8-8-8 or so at the rate of ½ to 1 pound for each year the tree is old up to a maximum of 8 pounds a year. Divide this into January and June applications.

A new persimmon should be pruned back to 2½ to 3 feet. Prune all but five or six shoots per foot of trunk to form a well-balanced tree. And that should about do it for pruning except for dead, interfering or broken branches—unless you get a particularly heavy fruit set, in which case you may want to do some thinning or bracing.

Persimmons have the bad habit of occasionally dropping their fruit—seemingly to compensate for over-vigorous vegetative growth. Try cutting back on nitrogen. Young trees tend to drop fruit readily when under stress; older trees tend to hold onto fruit that has already set.

PETUNIAS

A cold-hardy winter flower. Set plants (almost impossible to start from seed) October through February, pinch spent blooms, and petunias will keep producing through May or June. If—when is more like it—they get spindly, cut back to six inches or so; they'll rebound in no time. Often sold in multi-pots of three or four plants per pot. One of the basic winter flowers, along with pansies and snapdragons—and, in warmer parts, calendulas.

PHLOX

Many of the open roads here in Marion County (presumably in other counties, too) are lined with dwarf pink, purple and white phlox—and occasionally you see a whole pasture of it, which is an unforgettable sight. It blooms late February early-March through June, and it transplants well. If you'd feel a little uneasy digging it, you can get the closely-related *Phlox drummondii* seeds at many garden stores. I planted some when we first moved in, transplanted a few plants when the topsoil came—and now they've reseeded themselves and spread and spread, come up in February and bloom like crazy in March. The tall phlox, backbone of the perennial border, is listed as growing as far south as Zone 9, but you hardly ever (maybe never) see any.

PHOTINIA (RED-TIP, RED-TOP)

A fast-growing, evergreen shrub often used to screen utility boxes, refuse cans, heat pumps and such. New leaves are a surprisingly bright red, turning to shiny green as they mature. Has only moderate salt tolerance, likes organically enriched soil and full sun. Requires more or less constant pruning in the landscape and is subject to blackspot (easily controlled with Daconil). A favorite with new arrivals.

PINEAPPLES

We're a little too far north for pineapples, but you can still have some fun with them.

Next time you get one, leave a little extra (two to four inches) when you cut off the top. Let it dry for a day, then pot in sandy propagating soil. Keep warm and moist, and roots will develop quickly. You won't get another pineapple for a couple of years or so, but you will have a decorative, interesting bromeliad plant—related, oddly enough, to the Spanish moss so common here.

I have a neighbor who transplanted his pineapples into his garden, where they survived two nights of 17° F with the help of a covering sheet.

PINES

There are not that many pine or pine-like trees that grow in Florida. Three that are recommended are:

Sand Pine. A short-leaf pine with 3-inch needles in bundles of two. Egg-shaped cones two to 3½ inches. Native, fast growing, and comparatively small at 15 to 20 feet with a foot-thick trunk. Does well in poor, dry, sandy soil. Very sensitive to construction damage. Young specimens make good Christmas trees. Tip moth, scale and mushroom root rot the major pests.

Slash Pine. Needles 7 to 12 inches in bundles of 2 or 3. Native, fast growing—up to 90 feet with a 2 to 3-foot diameter. Three to 4½ inch cones fall in autumn. A good shade tree; also planted to stabilize soil, of which it tolerates a wide variety. Problems include pine pitch canker, sawflies, bark beetles and rust.

Spruce Pine. Native to northwest Florida's rich hammock soils. 3-inch needles in bundles of 2. Roundish cones 2 to 3½ inches. Medium growth rate, up to 100 feet and 2½-foot diameter. A beautiful tree often used in Bonsai. Bark beetle the commonest pest.

For the record, other Florida pines are:

Loblolly Pine. Six to 9-inch needles in bundles of 3. Two to

6-inch cones. 90 to 100 feet. An important hardwood pine (no softwood pines native to Florida) timber tree.

Longleaf Pine. Widely found (together with the turkey oak) in Florida's upland sandhills. Needles 8 to 18 inches in 3's (5's in some Gulf regions) with 6 to 10 inch cones. Important for lumber, pulp and (in the old days) resin.

Pond Pine. 6 to 8-inch needles in 3's, occasionally 4's. Usually grows in moist to swampy places.

Shortleaf Pine. 3 to 5-inch needles, usually in 2's. Up to 100 feet tall and 3 feet in diameter. An important timber tree.

PLUMBAGO

One of my favorite plants. A sprawling, unruly four to five foot shrub that dies back (here, anyway) in winter, but comes back quickly to produce, almost endlessly, pale blue one-inch flowers throughout the summer. You can use it as a color mass, as an informal hedge, or just by itself out in the noon-day sun.

POCKET GOPHERS

The first time I saw a string of gopher mounds—about eight inches high, a foot and more in diameter, zigging and zagging one after the other maybe six feet apart—I was mystified.

Now I know the pocket gopher for what he is—a nine to twelve inch premier pest, especially in your lawn. He tunnels his way looking for roots and tubers, and every now and then has to get rid of the excavated sand—hence the mounds. I have a neighbor who sits by the newest mound, and when the gopher kicks up a little more sand, wham, in goes the spade about a foot below where the sand came up. He's gotten several that way.

The more usual way to deal with gophers (who luckily are solitary animals—when you get one, there's not another in the tunnel to take its place) is to trap them; poisons, baits, exhaust fumes, etc., just don't work. Dig down in the newest mound until you hit the gopher's tunnel and set two traps (make sure the traps are tied to a gopher-proof anchor) one facing each way in the tunnel. In short order the gopher will show up to find out what's wrong with his tunnel, and chances are you've got him. Gopher traps are available at most garden stores.

PODOCARPUS

A member of the yew family, and it looks it. For a manicured hedge, one of your best choices. Evergreen. Takes full shade or partial sun, but needs well-drained soil. Tall, not too bushy growth, which makes it an ideal corner or accent shrub—or small tree, up to 40 feet, if you let it go. Two varieties: the fern (*P. gracilior*) is best limited to warmer areas; the yew variety (*P. macrophyllus*) does well anywhere. Occasionally susceptible to leaf spot, crown gall and dieback.

POINSETTIAS

If you live in central or near-central Florida, instead of tossing your Christmas poinsettia, try planting it. Choose a sunny, protected spot away from street and house lights (which confuse poinsettias about when to bloom), trim back about a third and plant when no more frost danger. Fertilize with 6-6-6 or 8-8-8 when new growth starts, again in June and once more in late fall. If heavy rains after the June-dose, better come again in July. When new growth reaches about a foot, cut back to four leaves per shoot. Keep repeating through the end of August to get a compact plant with lots of color—but don't prune after September 1. If a frost comes along, your poinsettia will know it, but will come back even stronger next year. Whiteflies and leaf disease are the major (but not that major) problems. Cygon or malathion and a copper fungicide should handle them. Incidentally, poinsettias make good cut flowers. Dip the cut in hot water for a minute, then plunge into cold to coagulate the milky sap and reduce wilting. Cut 24 hours ahead of time and keep in cool, draftless place until using.

PORTULACA

Also known as Rose Moss. A couple of packets of seed planted as fill-ins have been filling in for four years now, thanks to self-seeding. In spring and early summer, a mass of low-to-the-ground color. A little less profuse after that, but keeps on blooming until frost. The charts say to plant seed April through July; the self-seeded stuff starts to bloom in late March.

POTATOES

WHITE. Plant January-March in the north, January-February in central—or when seed potatoes show up in your garden store. The usual varieties are Kennebec and Red Pontiac, though Sebago, Atlantic, Red La Sorda, La Rouge and Superior are also recommended. Cut seed (store potatoes have been treated not to sprout) into about two-ounce sections with eyes on each section. The books say let the cut pieces harden for a few days; I've always shaken them with sulfur dust, planted right away and never had a problem. Space them about a foot apart and a trowel-blade deep.

A sense of the ridiculous is helpful with potatoes. My first year I got hit with early blight (little reddish dots on the leaves—had no idea what to do about them—maneb turns out to be a good answer) and the leaves just withered away. When it came time to plant something else, I suddenly started turning up potato after potato, and came away with about three gallons of them. The next year an early frost (17°) killed some of the foliage, from which the Red Pontiacs bounced back quickly and the Kennebecs slowly. Then another 17° came along, and just the opposite happened. Except for things like that, potatoes are easy to grow, and so much better than treated store potatoes.

SWEET. March-June north and February-June central. Sweet potato weevils are a serious problem—start with certified-free transplants, and use vine cuttings to prolong the growing season. Porto Rico, Georgia Red, Jewel, Centennial, Coastal Sweet and Boniato are recommended.

POWDER-POST BEETLES

Name for various small beetles that attack seasoned wood. Usually noticed by fine, powder-like sawdust. Look for them in unfinished floors, sub-flooring, floor joists, walls, furniture, stored wood in garages.

You can control them by spraying or brushing Dursban, with a second application in six to eight weeks. You won't kill buried beetles, but you will get emerging beetles and thus prevent re-infestation.

PRUNING

I always thought pruning was something you did to control size and shape. Then we moved to Florida, and a trio of crape myrtles opened my eyes to the why's and when's of pruning.

You prune to remove dead, dying, damaged and soon-to-be-damaged (such as when branches or limbs cross and rub each other) wood.

You prune to remove, and thus stop the spread of, diseased wood—and dip shears into a 9-parts-water, one-part-bleach solution in between cuts and before going on to the next plant.

Each pruning of young shrubs encourages branching and fullness—and on young trees helps single-trunk or leader formation.

You pinch blooms and prune weak fruits to increase fruit size—and, with peaches, for instance, to keep from overloading the branch.

You prune flowering shrubs (my crape myrtles) to get more and larger blossoms—pinch during the growing season to produce even more blooms—and lop developing seed heads to prolong the blooming season.

You prune to stimulate growth and increase plant vigor.

You prune worn out old plants in hopes of rejuvinating them—take out the worst third now, the next third next year, and the final third two years from now.

With some plants (peaches, again) you prune to let in more sunshine and improve air circulation.

The when's are just as important as the why's.

You can lightly prune trees and shrubs any time.

Best time to prune flowering shrubs is just after they finish blooming, unless you don't care about pruning off next year's blooms. To get more blooms next year, pinch new shoots up until a couple of months after blooming.

Most trees don't need pruning, but if you want to tidy up oaks, maples, sycamores or other large shade trees, the dormant season is the time to do it. Pruning at other times may promote undesirable sprouting.

The time to prune fruit trees (and grapes) is also during the dormant season. Prune blueberries after harvest.

As a rule, don't prune in late fall—you'll stimulate growth that may not have a chance to harden before frost. Exceptions are the evergreens (podocarpus, pittosporum, ligustrun, wax myrtle, boxwood, junipers, etc.) which you can prune any time.

For bushier, more compact pines, pinch back half the candle in spring, just before its needles expand. If you pinch at any other time, new buds won't form.

To encourage rapid shoot development and greater overall growth, prune shrubs just before the first spring growth. To retard growth, prune just after the spring growth flush.

Plants that produce flowers on new growth should be pruned towards the end of the dormant season. These include allamanda, abelia, hibiscus, roses, oleander, plumbago, cassia, crape myrtle and golden rain trees—to name just a few.

Wounds from pruning heal quickest if you prune just before or just after the spring growth flush. The pendulum keeps swinging on whether to use pruning paint or not. Right now it's not. Another pendulum: Do you prune at transplanting to compensate for root loss? Again, the current answer is no.

Pruning is easiest if done on a routine basis, with shears always in your pocket. It's also easier if you choose plants that don't need much pruning. Plant a photinia next to your foundation—it'll shoot up to 20 to 30 feet—and you'll be pruning it for the rest of your life.

How do you prune? Your county agent has specifics for quite a few plants. But the best way is to look at your plant, figure out what you'd like it to be and do, and go to it. I promise you, the first cut is the hardest—and from there on it's all down hill.

PYRACANTHA-SEE FIRETHORN

RADISHES

September to March both north and central. Cherry Belle, Comet, Early Scarlet Globe, White Icicle, Sparkler, Red Prince and Champion all do well.

REDBUD

Native tree to north and central Florida—and on up to the Canadian border. Small, pink-to-magenta flowers crowd the branches well before the leaves come out, providing some of our most spectacular, earliest color. Member of the pea family. 25 to 50 feet tall, deciduous, heart-shaped leaves, medium growth rate. Does best in full sun on fertile, well-drained soil. Major pests are canker disease and leaf spot fungi.

RED TIP—SEE PHOTINIA

ROSE MOSS—SEE PORTULACA

ROSES

Here in Florida, roses should live for six to eight years, grow and bloom for nine months of the year (north) to twelve months (central), with five bloom flushes a year (north) to seven in central Florida, with a few random blooms in between flushes.

In return, you'll have to spray and water weekly, groom and fertilize after each flush (some people fertilize monthly), prune in January and mulch as needed. Winter protection is not necessary, but you'll probably have to stake or trellis against the wind.

Fortuniana and Dr. Huey are the root stocks to look for. Roses are graded: Grade # 1 is best of the bare-roots, and Florida Fancy on Fortuniana of the container-grown. Allow a little more space between plants than up north. Plant bare-roots in December or January in north Florida, whenever available in central Florida. Plant container-grown any time, being careful not to disturb the roots. Roses need at least six hours of full sun, and morning sun is better than afternoon sun since it will dry the dew. Mix about ⅓ peat moss or compost in the hole to a depth of about a foot.

Rotate fertilizers—an 8-8-8, say, then a low-phosphate such as 10-0-10, two pounds or less per 100 square feet, depending on the nitrogen content. Or you can use something like a 13-4-6 routinely. Iron is the most common mineral deficiency, and iron sulfate is the remedy.

It's a good idea to rotate sprays, too. If you have only one or two plants, you're probably best off with an aerosol rose spray. If you have more, try rotating Daconil or Benomyl with Funginex for black spot and powdery mildew, and add some diazinon for thrips and mites. Most people spray once a week.

Roses need about an inch of water a week (more in hot-summer sandy-soil) either by rain or hose. If by hose, try to water the day before you spray to minimize foliage stress—and the less water you get on the leaves, the better.

Prune faded flowers, below-the-graft suckers and dead wood regularly. The big pruning comes in December (central) or January (north). Leave at least half of each main cane (except for climbers, which seem to do best when pruned down to about a foot), and expect first flowers on new wood in eight or nine weeks. Make cuts just above a dormant bud, and back to five-leaflet leaves.

SAGO PALM

The sago palm is not a palm, and it produces no sago—but for my money it's easily Florida's most pleasing foliage plant.

The sago is a cycad, a member of the most ancient plant family still living. It grows slowly, but in three or four years the growth is impressive. When our thermometer dropped to 12°, our sagos lost their fronds, but they grew back just fine come spring. If older fronds turn yellow, try spraying a tablespoon of magnesium sulfate (epsom salts) per gallon of water. If fronds turn brown and crinkly or frizzy, try a teaspoon of manganese sulfate per gallon. Fertilizing with a 10-5-5, or similar, two or three times a year will help things along.

ST. AUGUSTINEGRASS

Again from the UF's FLORIDA LAWN CARE, St. Augustinegrass produces a dark green, dense turf that is well adapted to most soils and climate conditions in Florida. It has good salt tolerance, and certain cultivars will generally tolerate shade better than other warm-season turfgrasses. Establishment of St. Augustine from sod (seeds just don't come true) is quick and easy. Several different cultivars of St. Augustine sod and plugs are available from garden centers and custom sod installers throughout Florida.

On the down side, St. Augustine, like most turfgrasses, has certain cultural and pest problems which may limit its use in some situations. The coarse leaf texture (looks like northern crab grass) is objectionable to some people. It requires irrigation to produce a good quality turf and does not retain green during drought conditions without supplemental irrigation. Excessive thatch buildup can occur under moderate to high fertility and frequent irrigation conditions. It has poor wear tolerance, and some varieties are susceptible to cold damage. The major insect pest of St. Augustine is chinch bug, but cultivar resistance is available (Floratam, Floralawn).

SCALE INSECTS AND MEALYBUGS

Scale insects cause more damage to more ornamentals than any other pests—and most ornamentals are attacked by one or more scale species.

Scales do their damage by sucking juices out of plants.

Heavily infested plants look unhealthy and produce little new growth. Scales feeding on the undersides of leaves may cause yellow spots on the top sides, which grow larger as the scales continue to feed. If scales are not controlled, leaves will drop prematurely and parts of twigs and branches can be killed.

Scales are classified as armored scales, soft scales and mealybugs.

Armored scales secrete a waxy covering over (but not part of) their bodies which protects them as they live and feed underneath. They run $1/16$ to $1/8$ of an inch in diameter and come in many colors. Female scales may be round, oval, oblong or pear-shaped. Mature males are tiny, wingless, gnat-like insects you almost never see. Tea Scales, Florida Red Scales and Oleander Scales are all armored scales.

Soft scales also secrete a waxy covering, but in their case it's attached to the body. Soft scales range from $1/8$ to $1/2$ inch, may be nearly flat to almost spherical in shape. Color varies widely. Examples are Brown Soft Scales, Hemispherical Scales, Japanese Scales and Florida Wax Scales.

Mealybugs resemble small wads of cotton, are usually found in leaf axils and are especially partial to cacti and succulents. They have no protective covering, and, unlike the armored and soft scales which spend all their adult lives in one place, mealybugs can move about.

Soft scales and mealybugs (also whiteflies and aphids) excrete large amounts of honeydew which attracts ants and sooty mold fungi. If you see ants or sooty mold, inspect for scale—also for whiteflies and aphids.

Scale eggs usually hatch when spring growth is at its peak.

Highly susceptible plants such as camellias, hibiscus and holly should be sprayed shortly after new growth hardens and before new scales mature. Spray again two weeks later. Spray to the point of run-off, and be sure to get the undersides of leaves. Best time to spray is in the cooler parts of the day to avoid spray-burn damage, and it's also good practice to water or irrigate ornamentals a day or two before spraying.

For mealybugs and immature scales in the crawling stage,

diazinon or Orthene is recommended. For mature armored and soft scales, you may want a systemic such as Cygon or Di-Syston, both of which can be applied as a soil drench. Oil sprays (such as Volck Oil) and malathion/oil spray can be effective against all forms of scale.

NOTE: Many species of scale are destroyed by tiny wasp-like parasites. If you see (with the help of a magnifying glass) scales with very small pin-prick holes in them, they've been parasitized. Try to delay using a pesticide to give the parasites a chance to exercise natural control.

SCORPIONS

Flattened, crab-like, ten legs and an upturned tail with a stinger at the tip, but a much tamer stinger than many people imagine. If you provoke or disturb it, the scorpion will use his stinger. Your wound may be swollen and painful for a few days, but no Florida scorpion can kill you. Scorpions are 1 to 4 inches, live outside (though they do occasionally come inside), hide under boards and such and are most active at night. They eat insects, spiders and other small creatures. Best thing to do with indoor scorpions is swat them with a shoe. You can treat their hiding areas with diazinon or malathion. And if you really want to get rid of them, keep a few chickens or ducks.

SHASTA DAISY

Easy to grow from seed, and kind of fun to think you can get a nice perennial like that for next to nothing. The catch is, they don't do well here, at least for me. Too darned hot, even partially shaded by the crape myrtles. The gloriosa daisy, on the other hand—we have a neighbor who grows it like weeds and can't give it away fast enough.

SILVERBELL

A small (to 25 feet), north Florida native tree with a wide-spreading, rounded crown on a short trunk. Leaves are light green above, even paler below, deciduous. Slow grower. Puts out small, bell-shaped, white flowers in spring. Does best in partial shade on fertile soils. A pretty little tree that should be more widely planted—and with no serious pests.

SNAPDRAGONS

The third pillar of the winter flower garden—the other two being pansies and petunias. Sold seasonally in multi-pots and (sometimes) bundles of 25. I've planted only the tall snapdragons—the Rockets—which are a bit slow taking hold but then make up for it. May occasionally need staking. Much easier to set out plants than to try to grow from seed. Plant October to December, cut spent stalks, and you should have color until May or June.

SOCIETY GARLIC

A native of south Africa not recommended for north Florida, but which seems to do very well here in Ocala. Plant bulbs (or container plants) any time of year in full sun, six to eight inches apart—and enjoy little purple flowers rising above one-foot, grass-like foliage on two-foot stems spring through fall. But pass one under your nose before you plunge—they do have a faint garlic odor that some people find objectionable.

SOD WEBWORMS

Small, dingy brown moths (wing span about ¾ of an inch) lay eggs in your lawn, and six weeks or more later (as early as April in south Florida, August in north Florida) tiny, greenish caterpillars with lots of black dots emerge and start chewing at the surface of your grass blades, leaving a colorless, membranous area. They hatch only 1/25th of an inch, then eat themselves up to ¾ of an inch when mature. They curl up on soil surface during the day and feed only at night or during cloudy, rainy periods. You can check for their presence by adding 1½ ounces of hand dishwashing liquid to a 2-gallon sprinkler can of water and drenching a four square foot area. If sod webworms are present, they'll start crawling and you can see them.

You'll often notice sod webworms first along hedges and flower beds. A few spots, maybe two to three feet across, turn a ragged yellowish-brownish. These spots can fuse and grow larger. In extreme cases, sod webworms can kill your grass— but if you keep it well watered, it should come back.

Good lawn management (slow-release fertilizers, don't cut too short, ¾ to 1 inch of water a week) can help control sod webworms—and control with pesticides is quite easy. The insecticide of choice is *Bacillus thuringienses,* a bacterium that kills only caterpillars and goes under the name of Dipel, BT or Thuricide. You can also spread granular diazinon, Dursban or Sevin and water lightly, about ⅛ inch. And, often, no need to treat the whole lawn—you can spot-treat damaged areas plus a 10-foot buffer zone.

SOIL pH

Since plants can't take solid food, the solubility—and thus availability—of plant nutrients is important. Some plant nutrients (and some plant poisons) that are soluble at one pH are insoluble at another pH.

That said, the best single thing to do about Florida soil pH is—relax. Most plants have far wider pH tolerance than the books and "desirable pH range" charts give them credit for. As a rule of thumb, if your pH is within 0.4 of "ideal", don't meddle with it.

Most Florida soils have a pH between 5.5 and 6.8, which is ideal for growing most things. If your pH is considerably higher (due to naturally occurring limestone, marl, sea shells or waste concrete/mortar at construction sites), there's not much you can do. One pound of elemental sulfur per one hundred square feet can lower pH one unit, but only temporarily. With specimen plants, better to dig a hole a foot deep by 10 inches wide near the drip line, mix two or three tablespoons of sulfur with the soil and put it back. Repeated annually, even such a small amount of acidified soil can help a shrub or small tree ward off nutrient deficiency. A heavy application of manure, compost or peat can help some plants overcome too-high pH.

If your soil pH is in the low 5's, three pounds of limestone (or even better, dolomite limestone—a little magnesium is always welcome) per 100 square feet can raise the pH half a unit or so. Apply two to three months before planting, repeat from time to time—but never without a soil test first to make sure you need it.

Landscape plants known to prefer below pH 5.5 include azaleas, bahiagrass (ours does OK at 6.7), ixora, partridgeberry, phlox (again, ours does OK at 6.7) and blue hydrangea. Those known to prefer 6.0 or higher include ash, butterfly bush, elm, pink hydrangea, red cedar, sycamore and yucca. If the species you're interested in isn't listed here, chances are it'll do fine whatever soil you give it.

SOOTY MOLD

Aphids, whiteflies and some scales deposit a sweet substance called honeydew which attracts ants (which virtually farm aphids) and a black, sheetlike fungus called sooty mold—because it looks so like a layer of soot on leaf surfaces. If you see ants or sooty mold on your plants, check for (mainly) aphids. Sooty mold doesn't harm plants, but you may find it unsightly. Easiest way to get rid of it is to wash it off with 1½ ounces liquid soap or detergent per gallon of water—or sometimes just hose it off.

SPANISH MOSS

A much-misunderstood plant. An air plant that gets its nourishment from rainwater and air, and probably from dust, as well. Spanish moss uses the tree only for support (witness you see it growing on power lines), though it may occasionally weigh down an old limb or smother a new, small one.

Spanish moss puts forth a pretty little purplish flower which produces a feathery seed that wind-blows until it lands on a limb, a trunk, whatever.

Up until after World War II Spanish moss was used for stuffing furniture; the last plant burned down in 1958. The moss has a reputation for harboring chiggers. Moss that fell in damp, low places, yes. But moss that hangs a few feet or more above the ground, almost never.

Ball moss—small, tufted, soft, greenish gray—is related and often found on the same tree. Both, by the way, are bromeliads, related to the pineapple.

SPINACH

A cool weather crop. Sow October-November both north and central. Virginia Savory, Dixie Market, Hybrid 7 and that old stand-by Bloomsdale Longstanding are all recommended.

SQUASH - Summer

With luck, a two-season crop. Plant March-April in the north, then again August-September. Central dates are February-March, August-September. I've had zucchini die down in the summer, then come back in the fall and produce until frost. Fruit rot is a common problem, caused by a fungus and incomplete pollination. Recommended varieties are Early Prolific Straightneck, Dixie, Summer Crookneck, Cocozelle, Gold Bar, Zucchini, Peter Pan, Sundrops, Scallopini and Sunburst.

SQUASH - Winter

March in the north, February-March in central. Sweet Mama, Table Queen, Butternut and Spaghetti are recommended.

STRAWBERRIES

Strawberries are grown as annuals in all parts of Florida. Set them out September 15 through November 15. Freezing won't harm the plants, but it may injure or kill flowers and fruits, which will come again later. Plants will produce until longer days and warmer weather turn their energy to putting out runners instead of fruit. You can set the runners to produce plants for next fall, but best to swap them with a neighbor as a form of mini crop rotation.

Most soils will do, with well-drained-moist-and-sandy the best and muck and peat (Florida peat) the worst. Broadcast 6-6-6 or 8-8-8 at the rate of two and a half pounds per 100 square feet and work it in. Side-dress as (and if) needed. Spread the roots fan-shape and set so the crown isn't covered but the root tops are. Mulching is in order, and black plastic makes an excellent one.

Here in Marion County, the variety Sequoia seems to give the best results to the most people. Other recommended varieties are Florida 90 and Florida Belle. Everbearing varieties are *not* recommended.

The only real pest problem I've run into is birds, especially mocking birds, which a hardware cloth cage (for a very small bed) or netting takes care of. Other problems can include thrips, spider mites, slugs, leaf and stem spots, blight and fruit rot.

SULFUR, Dusting

A fungicide/insecticide for use as a dust or spray on certain ornamentals, vegetables, fruit and citrus trees. Also good against chiggers. See the label for particulars.

One of the few "cides" available to the organic gardener.

SWEET GUM

One of our finest native trees. 60 to 80 feet tall with (usually) a straight trunk and a conical crown. Has deep red fall foliage—not that common here. Completely cold hardy—as far north as Connecticut, in fact. Happiest in moist, rich soil, but will accept almost anything you give it, including dry soil. Drops spiny seed balls (about an inch and a half in diameter— you don't want to step on them barefoot) and leaves, but not that much messier than most trees. An excellent, fast growing shade tree. Subject to something called bleeding necrosis (oozing sap flow, more a nuisance than a problem) and scale (which you'd treat only in a small, young tree).

SYCAMORE

A fast growing, native shade tree that can reach 80 to 100 feet. Usually grows along creek beds, but is not particular and can even take considerable drought. Kind of messy in the fall when it drops its leaves (I believe it's the largest-leaf north American native shade tree) and seed balls (source of itching powder when I was a boy) and sheds its bark, which is normal. Susceptible to lace bugs in the fall—but leaves are about to drop anyway, so no need to do anything.

TERMITES

Come in two unpleasant forms—drywood and subterranean. You can tell both from ants easily: ants have waists, termites don't.

Drywoods live in just that—dry wood—and have no contact with soil. They swarm all year round but mostly January to May, and that's when they establish new colonies. Best ways to keep them out are screens all around, especially in the attic; paint all exposed wood; fill cracks and crevices; and use pressure-treated lumber whenever possible. The only way to treat a bad infestation is to have a licensed pest control company tent your house and fumigate.

Subterranean termites are much more common. They nest in soil, from which they get moisture, and feed on wood—also on paper, fibreboard and some natural fibres. These are the ones who build tunnels to get from the soil to your house. It's a good idea to check for these tubes at least once a year, preferably in summer.

Best prevention is to break contact between soil and wood. You can do it yourself—dig a trench 6 to 12 inches deep and 4 to 6 inches wide and apply diluted (see label) pesticide at rate of one gallon every five feet if you have a foundation, two gallons per five feet if on a cement slab—or call in the pest controller.

A particularly destructive subterranean termite is the Formosan variety, introduced in Texas in 1965 and now well established in Florida. This one swarms in April and May.

If you have a subterranean infestation, no need to panic—a couple of weeks, or even a month, won't make much difference. Take a few specimens to your county agent to find out the variety, then get estimates.

All termites are attracted to light. If you can't obtain specimens, look for discarded wings on lighted window sills, and take these to your county agent.

TICKS

We have two basic ticks—the brown dog tick, which is an indoor and outdoor pest, and the American tick, which lives strictly outdoors.

A well-fed female brown dog tick will lay up to 3000 eggs in a mass. The eggs hatch into seed ticks so small you won't see them unless they bunch together. Seed ticks attach to your dog, take a blood meal, remain attached for three to six days, turn bluish, fall off, hide for a couple of weeks and molt into an eight-legged reddish-brown nymph. They're now ready for another meal, after which they drop off again, molt again, this time into reddish-brown adults which seek yet another meal, turn bluish and swell up to about ⅓ inch—and the cycle repeats. They can live long periods at any of these stages without feeding—up to 200 days for adults.

The American dog tick goes through much the same stages, except that it feeds on rodents instead of dogs up until the final stage. Larvae can live 540 days without food, nymphs up to 584 days, and adults up to two years.

The brown dog tick carries no known human diseases; the American dog tick can carry Rocky Mountain spotted fever, tularemia and other diseases. If you're bitten, early removal of the tick is important since disease organisms aren't trans-ferred until the tick has fed for several hours. The American dog tick can also cause paralysis in dogs and children when they attach at the base of the skull or along the spinal column. Fortunately, when the tick is removed, recovery is rapid, usually within eight hours.

Ticks can easily be removed by touching with a hot needle or a swab of alcohol. A small dab of skin attached to the tick's mouth is normal. Sevin dust or malathion dust will help control ticks on your pet—Baygon, malathion, diazinon or Sevin outdoors—and Baygon or diazinon indoors. For a severly infested pet, a dip is in order.

THRIPS

Can be very common in Florida. Tiny, rasping/sucking insects on leaves and flowers, especially roses, where they turn petal tips brown and shrively. Best way to check for them is to shake vigorously a suspected leaf (may look anything from pimply to having little air bubbles) or flower over a sheet of white paper. If near-microscopic specks fall out and start walking, that's thrips. Malathion now, and again in seven to ten days, is recommended. You can also use Orthene or Cygon.

TOMATOES

Tomatoes are Florida's most important commercial vegetable, but that doesn't make them easy to grow, at least here in Ocala. If you set plants out early (February in the north, January in central) they run the chance of freezing. If you set them out late (April, March), they'll probably run into hot weather just as they start producing—and stop setting new fruit as temperatures go over 85°. According to the books, you can set fall plants in August (north) and September (central)—but most of the gardeners I know don't bother any more.

A partial answer to this is to plant a little later with larger plants—not the garden store ones forced in the green-house, but from seeds started 8 to 10 weeks before (instead of the usual 6 to 8 weeks) and up-potted as needed. Better Boy and Celebrity are favored varieties around here, but the garden stores carry quite a few others and chances are they'll do fine. The more F's, V's, N's and such on the label (resistant to fusarium and verticillum wilts and nematodes) the better. Cutworms are a problem—a collar or piece of aluminum foil wrapped around the stem just below and above ground level is a good idea. Blossom end rot is caused by calcium deficiency—calcium chloride foliar spray is the remedy. For early blight, late blight and other leaf spots, try maneb. For hornworms, I like to spray lightly with a pyrethrin aerosol, and when the hornworms start swaying, scissor them in half. Not much you can do about sunscald, cracking and blossom drop.

Beyond those, tomatoes really don't suffer much from pests and disease.

I've learned three new tomato words since coming to Florida: Indeterminate—regular size tomatoes, vines keep growing after fruit sets, should be staked. Determinate—smaller fruit, tends to ripen all at once, doesn't need staking. And indetermediate—mostly cherry tomatoes, suit yourself as to staking. I cage my tomatoes, and it doesn't seem to matter much if I pinch the suckers or not. A little superphosphate mixed into the bottom of the hole seems to pay dividends, but no guarantees. Five pounds of 6-6-6 or 8-8-8 per 100 square feet at planting, a good side dressing about three weeks after planting, then light side dressings every ten days or so should take care of fertilizer needs, and watered in is better than just left on top. Give them an inch of water a week, ideally by soaker hose or drip irrigation. Mulch is recommended. Less than fully ripe tomatoes (like bananas) should be kept out of the refrigerator.

TRUMPET VINE

In three years, with zero care, a two-foot, pencil-thin trumpet vine grew to take over our entire front wall. You often see them growing on old stumps along the road. A native plant that comes in the usual orange or in yellow. I've seen them attract hummingbirds up north, but (so far) not here.

TULIP POPLAR

Also called just plain tulip tree, or (sometimes) the yellow poplar—though it isn't a poplar at all, but related to the magnolias. The "tulip" comes from its large, greenish-yellow (with traces of pink) tulip-shaped flowers. A fast grower, up to 80 feet, with surprisingly few (or no) lower branches. A beautiful, native tree with striking yellow fall color. Old specimens are kind of dirty, dropping twigs and branches— but has no serious pests. Deciduous.

TURNIPS

Fortunately, my wife and I both like turnips—it would be a pity not to like something that grows so well. Six or eight feet of Purple Top White Globe, best done in two sowings, September and October, will give you a turnip a week from December to March. If you're really fond of turnips, you can put in a spring crop from January through March. I've tried rutabagas side by side with Purple Tops—for whatever reason, they did next to nothing.

WALNUT, Black

Not usually thought of as a shade tree, but a good one. Native. Does best on fertile, well drained soils. A medium-speed grower, up to 70 feet. If you can open them, the nuts are edible—kind of strong-tasting, so usually used for flavoring. A deciduous tree with no serious pests.

WATERMELON

March-April and July-August north; January-March and August central. Small varieties suggested unless you have a lot of garden space. Look for seeds resistant to fusarium wilt. Need bees for ·pollination. Large varieties are Charleston Gray, Jubilee, Crimson Sweet and Dixielee. Small: Sugar Baby, Minilee and Mickylee. A seedless variety, Fummy, is occasionally available—at a price.

WAX MYRTLE

One of our best native shrubs/small trees, ten to 20 feet tall. Grows in all 67 Florida counties. Cold hardy and evergrecn. Puts out small, wax-coated, bluish-green berries that attract wildlife. Leaves are small, aromatic when crushed. Moderate growth rate on wet or dry soil. Makes an excellent accent tree or a good, no-clipping-needed hedge or screen. Best started with small transplants. Pests include caterpillars and canker disease.

WHITEFLIES

Common on many ornamentals including citrus, gardenias and ligustrums, and also many annuals. If you shake a plant and a cloud of white flies up, that's whiteflies.

Whiteflies are only about $1/16$ inch long. Wings and body are covered with a fine white, powdery wax. Eggs are laid on the undersides of leaves and hatch into nymphs (crawlers) which are slightly smaller than the head of a pin, round in shape and light green to whitish and somewhat transparent. They remain on the leaf underside, insert their piercing/sucking beaks and suck out juices. In the Gainesville area, three major generations occur in late March, mid-June and late August. In northern Florida, tack on another week.

Whiteflies (along with soft scales, mealybugs and aphids) excrete honeydew, which attracts ants and makes an excellent medium for sooty mold fungus. If you notice ants or sooty mold, check for any of these sucking insects.

Some whitefly varieties are parasitized by a small wasp which does a pretty good job of controlling them. Parasitized nymphs (the parasites don't attack adult whiteflies) will contain the larva or pupa of the parasite or the emergence hole through which the parasite escaped. You'll need a magnifying glass to see these things.

If you don't find signs of parasitism, you can use quite a few things to control whiteflies—or help control them; some varieties can be quite difficult. Among them: soap solution, diazinon, oil spray, oil/malathion spray and Orthene. Spray plants to the point of run-off, and be sure to cover the undersides of leaves. Best to spray in late afternoon, and to have watered or irrigated a day or two before.

Two systemics also work against whiteflies. DiSyston granules and Cygon can both be applied as soil drenches. They won't work as fast as the sprays, but they'll work over a considerably longer period of, usually, six to eight weeks. They also have the added advantage of being relatively harmless to whitefly parasites.

WIREWORMS

You know those shiny, yellow/reddish-brown, hard, thin, jointed worms you sometimes dig up? Up to an inch and a half long? Most likely they're wireworms—larvae of the click beetle or dor—and they do you no good. They nibble at potatoes, carrots and other root crops, with an occasional side dish of bulbs, seedlings and the smaller roots of larger plants.

Deep tilling (to expose the worms to you and other predators) and tilling between rows of susceptible crops are two forms of control. Baiting is more fun. Plant nearly mature carrots, with greens still on, every three feet or so—pull them up every three days—pluck off the wireworms—re-insert the carrot.

ZEPHYR LILY

A very attractive, small lily. Enrich your soil with organic matter and plant bulbs September to March, one to two inches deep, three inches apart. White, yellow, red and pink blossoms spring to fall. Never any need to dig up and store. Like full sun to partial shade, and you can grow them as potted houseplants as well.

ZINNIAS

Another flower many native Floridians are not familiar with—largely because it invariably gets a leaf spot disease there's nothing you can do anything about except pull the plant and destroy it. But before the leaf spot gets the upper hand, you'll get several months of beautiful flowers. Well worth planting.

ZOYSIAGRASS

Every now and then (especially when the advertisements appear) you hear a lot about Zoysiagrass, and quite a few people send away for plugs. Let's see what the UF FLORIDA LAWN CARE has to say.

On the plus side, zoysia is adapted to a wide variety of soils and has good tolerance to shade and salt spray. It offers good to excellent wear resistance and provides an extremely dense sod which reduces weed invasion. Once established, its slow growth means less-frequent mowing. The density of a zoysia lawn is second to none and the uniformity is excellent. When properly maintained, zoysiagrasses make excellent lawns.

However, regardless of what the advertisements say, zoysias have disadvantages like all Florida turfgrasses. The improved zoysias have to be propagated vegetatively and are extremely slow in becoming established. Two growing seasons may be required for coverage of the lawn when propagated by plugging or sprigging. All zoysias form a heavy thatch which requires periodic renovation. Other disadvantages include slow recovery from damage, high fertility requirement, need for frequent irrigations, possible severe damage by nematodes, billbugs and several diseases. For maximum beauty, a reel mower must be used for cutting.

This is not so much a How To book (the author claims no green thumb) as a What Will book (he does admit to a green head).

The assumption is that you already know a good deal about gardening—or you wouldn't be standing there reading this. You already know how to plant a tree, when to dead-head the annuals or dig the potatoes—so no point going into all of that.

Instead, what "The Newcomer's Guide" tries to do is adapt what you already know to our strange north-central Florida climate. Take a look at the Contents At A Glance in front of the book. If you have any questions about a number of the topics covered—or would like to try your hand at some of them— we believe this may well be the guide for you.